The Veiled

Being an Account of the Risks and Adventures
Ahamadou, Sheikh of the Azjar Maraude

William Le Queux

Alpha Editions

This edition published in 2024

ISBN : 9789362921444

Design and Setting By
Alpha Editions
www.alphaedis.com
Email - info@alphaedis.com

As per information held with us this book is in Public Domain.
This book is a reproduction of an important historical work. Alpha Editions uses the best technology to reproduce historical work in the same manner it was first published to preserve its original nature. Any marks or number seen are left intentionally to preserve its true form.

Contents

Preface .... - 1 -
Chapter One. .... - 2 -
Chapter Two. .... - 16 -
Chapter Three. .... - 30 -
Chapter Four. .... - 47 -
Chapter Five. .... - 57 -
Chapter Six. .... - 67 -
Chapter Seven. .... - 78 -
Chapter Eight. .... - 85 -
Chapter Nine. .... - 95 -
Chapter Ten. .... - 103 -
Chapter Eleven. .... - 111 -

Preface.

Author's Note.

The remarkable adventures of the notorious robber-sheikh Ahamadou, "the Abandoned of Allah," once the terror of the Areg Desert, but now friendly to the French, were collected during a journey across the Great Sahara. In the belief that some description of the wild life of the Desert, with its romance and mystery, told by one upon whose head a price was set for twelve years, and who a dozen times narrowly escaped capture, may interest those fond of adventure, I have translated, edited, and presented these reminiscences in their present form.

Chapter One.

The City of the Seven Shadows.

During half a century of constant wandering over the silent sunlit sands, of tribal feuds, of revolts, battle and pillage, of bitter persistent hatreds, of exploit, foray, and fierce resistance against the lounging Spahis, cigarette-smoking Zouaves, black-faced Turcos, and swaggering Chasseurs of the French, I have met with some curious adventures, and have witnessed wonders more remarkable, perhaps, than many of the romances related by the Arab story-tellers. They mostly occurred before I was chosen sheikh of the Azjar; when I was simply one of a band of desert-pirates, whose only possessions were a long steel lance, a keen, finely-tempered poignard, and a white stallion, the speed of which was unequalled by those of my companions. A thief I was by birth; a scholar I had become by studying the *Tarik*, the *Miraz*, the *Ibtihadj*, and the Korân, under the Marabut Essoyouti in Algiers; a philosopher I fain would be. When riding over the great limitless redbrown sands, I was apt to forget the race whence I sprang, the learning that had made me wise, the logical reasonings of a well-schooled brain, and give myself up with all the rapture of an intense enthusiasm to the emotion of the hour. It was the same always. Essoyouti, a scholar renowned throughout Tripoli and Tunis, had versed me in legendary lore, until I had become full of glowing fancies and unutterable longing to penetrate the entrancing mysteries to which he had so often referred as problems that could never be solved.

I am a Veiled Man. Openly, I confess myself a vagabond and a brigand. Living here, in the heart of the Great Desert, six moons march from Algiers, and a thousand miles beyond the French outposts, theft is, with my nomadic tribe, their natural industry—a branch of education, in fact. We augment the meagreness of our herds by extorting ransoms from some of our neighbours, and completely despoiling others. Mention of the name of Ahamadou causes the face of the traveller on any of the caravan routes between the Atlas mountains and Lake Tsâd to pale beneath its bronze, for as sheikh of the most powerful piratical tribe in the Sahara, I have earned an unenviable notoriety as leader of "The Breath of the Wind," while the Arabs themselves have bestowed upon my people three epithets which epitomise their psychology: "Thieves, Hyenas, and Abandoned of Allah."

The only law recognised by my race, the Touaregs, is the right of the strongest. We wear the black *litham* wrapped about our faces, leaving only our noses and eyes visible, and never removing it, even at mealtimes. It becomes so much a part of us that any one being deprived of his veil is unrecognisable to friends or relatives. If one of our number is killed, and divested of his veil, no one can identify him until it has been restored to its place. We are therefore known and dreaded as "The Veiled Men."

My first journey by paths untrodden resulted strangely.

For two whole moons a party of us, numbering nearly three hundred, all well-armed and desperate, had been lurking in a narrow ravine in the far South, known as the Gueden, close to the point where it is crossed by the route taken by the caravans from Lake Tsâd to El Aghouat in Algeria. News travels fast in the desert. We had received word that a caravan laden with ivory and gold-dust was on its way from Kuka to Timissao, and were awaiting it, with the intention either of levying toll, or attacking it with a view to plunder. In our sombre robes of dark blue kano cloth and black veils, we were a mysterious, forbidding-looking rabble. As day succeeded day, and we remained inactive, with scouts ever vigilant for the approach of our prey, I recollected that in the vicinity were some curious rocks, with inscriptions recording the Mussulman conquest, and one morning, mounting my *meheri*, or swift camel, rode out to inspect them.

The sun rose, and beneath its furnace heat I pushed on into the great waterless wilderness of Tasili, the true extent of which is unknown even to us Children of the Desert, for the utter dearth of water there renders a journey of many days impossible. Until the *maghrib* hour I remained in the saddle, then dismounting, faced towards the Holy Ca'aba, recited my *fâtihat*, ate a handful of dates, and squatted to smoke and watch the fading of the blood-red afterglow. On the next day, and the next, I journeyed forward over the wide monotonous plain, where the poison-wind fanned my brow like a breath from an oven, and nothing met the aching eye but glaring sand and far-off horizon, until, when my shadow lengthened on the sixth day after parting with my companions, I found myself within sight of a range of high hills, looming darkly against the brilliant sunset.

Well acquainted as I was with the geography of my native sands, I had never heard mention of these hills, and was therefore convinced that I had mistaken the route to the great black rock whereon the inscriptions were engraved, and was now approaching a region unexplored. On many occasions I had traversed the caravan route to Timissao, and crossed the rocky ravine where my companions were now in ambush; but none of us had ever before left that track, clearly defined by its bleaching bones, for to the solitary traveller in that inhospitable region a pricked water-skin or a lame camel means death. With irrepressible awe I gazed upon the hills, clothed in the deep purple light of the descending sun, because of one strange thing my eyes had detected. I saw, above the serrated line, two cone-like peaks, rising close to one another, in majesty solemn and sublime, and recognised in them a scene exactly as described by my master Essoyouti, in one of the curious romances he was fond of relating. I stood recalling every detail of the scene, just as I had imagined it when, seated under the vine, in the cool patio of his house, in the ancient Kasbah at Algiers, he had told me a story that held me breathless and entranced.

Worn with fatigue, exhausted and feverish from long exposure to the fiery sun, half stifled by the sand-laden wind, and riding a camel scarcely less jaded than myself, I confess that, despite my love of adventure, and by reason of the strangeness of the story I had heard, I contemplated with no little dread the prospect of passing that night alone within sight of those twin mountain-crests. Twilight is brief in the desert, and soon the moon, having risen from behind a bank of cloud, afforded an uncertain light, which partly illuminated the prospect, and I sat hugging my knees and thinking deeply until sleep closed my eyes.

Before the appearance of the first saffron streak that heralds the sun's coming, I had recited a *sûra* and mounted, with my face set resolutely towards the unknown range. In the skin across my saddle I had only just sufficient water to enable me to return to our ambush, therefore I broke not my fast, determined to hoard up my frugal store. The sand was soft and treacherous. At every step my camel's spongy feet sank deeper and deeper, until, after a toilsome ride of three hours, we arrived near the foot of the two dark, ominous-looking mountains. Then I pulled up, fearing to proceed further lest we should be overwhelmed by the quicksands.

Near me was a narrow pass between the two mountains, and shading my eyes with my hand, I was startled at beholding two gigantic figures standing on either side of the entrance. The sight of them confirmed my suspicion that I had approached the Unknown, and with curiosity aroused, I urged my *meheri* still forward, coming at last close up to the colossal figures. They were fashioned from enormous blocks of dark grey stone, ten times the height of a human being. One, carved to represent a beautiful woman, had her right hand lifted towards the sky, while the other, a forbidding-looking hag, with chipped, time-worn face still wearing a repulsive expression, pointed downward. Between these colossal figures was a space of about thirty paces. According to the legend related by the sage Essoyouti, and told by our story-tellers through ages, there existed beyond a land forbidden.

I held my breath. I was about to view a country that had not been viewed; the ravine known in story as the Valley of the Ants. In eagerness I pressed onward, leading my camel, and passing up the stony valley until at length I came to a second and more fertile space of vast extent, covered entirely by the colossal ruins of a forgotten city.

Aghast, I stood gazing upon the remarkable and unexpected scene.

Ruined temples, with long rows of broken columns, and great houses cracked and fallen into decay, stood silent and deserted, grim, grey relics of a glorious past. Here and there obelisks and colossi still stood, and the broad streets of the giant city were everywhere well-defined by the ruins, half-buried by drifting sand on either side. Above, a single eagle soared high in the heavens, the only sign of life in that once populous and magnificent centre of a lost civilisation.

Having tethered my camel, I started forward through the ocean of soft sand that through centuries had drifted over the place, and as I did so the story of old Essoyouti recurred to me. The appearance of the place agreed with the strange legend in almost every detail. The ruler of this gigantic capital had been Balkîs, the wealthy and luxurious queen mentioned in our Book of Everlasting Will. This was actually the city of Saba, once the wealthiest and most magnificent capital in the world. According to the legend of the sages, this place existed somewhere in the Great Desert, but whereabouts no man had been able to determine, although it was believed that its entrance was between two cone-like mountains, but surrounded by quicksands of so treacherous a nature that none dare approach it.

With hurried footsteps I scrambled on over fallen columns and great blocks of hewn stone, with inscriptions in characters unknown to me, until suddenly my eyes were bewildered at beholding on the mountain-side an enormous palace, with beautiful terraces and pavilions, apparently in an excellent state of preservation. From the city it was approached by a long flight of wide stone steps, flanked on either side by a pair of colossal figures of similar design to those at the entrance of the Valley of the Ants.

At first, I doubted that the scene before me was one of actual reality, but having reassured myself that I was not dreaming, and was entirely in possession of my senses, I gripped my long lance firmly, and started to ascend the thousand steps that gave access to the historic palace of Balkîs. Hardly, however, had I placed my foot upon the first step, when my eyes were blinded by a lightning-flash, and my ears deafened by a crash of thunder, that, shaking the earth, resounded among the hills, until it became lost in innumerable echoes.

I halted in suspicion, puzzled to account for the strange phenomenon, which seemed like some ominous warning.

Nothing daunted, however, I sprang up the steps, two by two, halting but once to regain breath, and in a few minutes entered the great, marvellously-sculptured portals of the magnificent dwelling-place of one of the most powerful and beautiful women the world ever knew. About to enter, my footsteps were suddenly arrested by the discovery that the floor of the palace was of running water, wherein fish disported themselves, and in the centre, raised upon a daïs of ivory and gold, was the great empty throne of Balkîs, constructed entirely of chalcedony, amethysts, and rubies.

The extent of my discoveries entranced me. I twisted up my robe, and prepared to wade through the water, when, on setting foot into it, I discovered to my amazement that the floor was of transparent glass, laid over the running water, thus keeping the palace uniformly cool during the hottest hours. On approaching the throne I at once became aware of its enormous value, and with my poignard prised from its setting one of the largest rubies my eyes had ever beheld. It was the size of a pigeon's egg, and of matchless colour.

Through the wonderful courts of the deserted palace I wandered, amazed at every turn. Of gigantic proportions, with strange grotesque embellishments that clearly showed its ancient origin, it had stood here in the zenith of its magnificence ages before the days of the Prophet, and for many centuries had remained hidden from the sight of man within that unknown valley. From the flat roof of one of its pavilions I stood gazing down upon the once mighty city, trying to reconstruct it in my imagination, and endeavouring to form an idea of its aspect in the long-past days, when the hosts of Balkîs went forth to battle, and when the beautiful queen herself flashed forth in her golden chariot, amid the wild plaudits of the multitude.

Many hours I spent in exploring this wonderful relic of a decayed civilisation, visiting pavilion after pavilion and finding most of them knee-deep in the accumulated dust of ages, until at last I came to a small chamber built right against the side of the mountain. This I entered, finding traces of the most extravagant luxury within. The decorations were richly ornamented with gold even now untarnished, the beams supporting the roof being set with gems which sparkled where a ray of sunlight fell upon them. Beyond was a door which, on examination, proved to be of solid iron. On dragging it open there was disclosed a small, dark, and cavernous burrow into the mountain-side. Minutely I examined this door, and finding thereon great bolts with sockets sunk deeply into the solid rock, it occurred to me that in this place might be hidden some of the treasure that the Korân tells us was possessed by the great Queen Balkîs. Cupidity prompted me to search, and having constructed a large improvised torch, I propped open the door with a huge stone sculptured to represent a lion's paw, and started forward up the narrow gloomy tunnel. The natural sides of the cavern were rough, gleaming with long pendant stalactites; but soon it grew larger, and the air became so warm that the perspiration fell from my brow in big drops. One or two articles, old cross-hilted swords, a rusty, dinted helmet and a battered breastplate, showed that this place had long ago been frequented, therefore I pressed forward eagerly, hoping to discover that which would render me wealthy. The increasing heat within the cavern surprised me; nevertheless I went forward, my torch held high above my head, my eyes eagerly strained into the impenetrable gloom, and my feet stumbling ever and anon over the uneven ground, until suddenly a harsh grinding noise fell upon my ears, and next second a crushing blow fell full upon my skull, felling me like a log and rendering me unconscious.

How long I remained in that dark stifling tunnel I have no idea.

When, slowly and painfully, I opened my eyes I found that my veil had been removed, my brow deftly bandaged, and my fevered head was resting upon a woman's cool hand. A soft feminine voice gave me "Peace," and turning I saw by the light of a burning brazier that my companion was a girl of wondrous beauty. Her face was of the pure Arab type, her complexion white as those of the Englishwomen who come to Biskra at Ramadan; her little skull-cap was thickly embroidered with seed-pearls, and her bracelets and anklets, set with beautiful diamonds, gleamed with a thousand iridescent fires at each movement. At first I fancied myself dreaming, but when at length I entirely recovered consciousness, I recognised that we were together in a small apartment hung with heavy hangings of thick dark crimson stuffs. The golden perfuming-pan diffused an intoxicating odour of attar of roses, and the silken couch whereon I reclined was soft, restful, and spacious.

Turning to my companion who, instantly divining my longing, handed me water in a crystal goblet, I enquired where I was.

"Thou art with a friend," she answered. "Thou hast dared to enter the City of the Seven Shadows bent on plunder, and the wrath hath fallen upon thee."

"Didst thou discover me?" I asked, raising myself upon my elbow, and looking at her.

She nodded, and with bent head sat with her luminous dark eyes fixed upon the ground.

"Thou hast entered this, the city upon which the seven lights of the heavens have cast the shadows of their wrath, and where all who enter are accursed," she exclaimed at last, speaking slowly and impressively. "Thou earnest hither with evil intent, to secure the treasure of Balkîs. Yet out of evil cometh good, for in thee I have found a companion in adversity."

"In adversity!" I echoed. "What art thou?"

"I am Balkîs, sole lineal descendant of the great queen who ruled over Saba, and guardian of her treasure," she answered. "I am a queen without court; a ruler without people. The palace that thou hast inspected is mine; the throne from the arm of which thou hast filched the great ruby is my lonely seat of royalty; for I am queen of a dead city. Although I am bearer of the historic name of Balkîs, and possess treasure of greater worth than men have ever dreamed, my subjects number only fourteen persons, all of whom are my relatives and live here with me in this my palace. As thou hast already seen, our once-powerful city with its fifty brazen gates hath fallen into decay because of the curse placed upon it by Allah. The teeming populace that once crowded its thoroughfares and market-places have dwindled down until mine own family only are left, the last of a long illustrious, world-famed line. Soon, alas! I, too, shall pass into the grave, and the royal house of Balkîs will become extinct," and her jewel-laden breast rose and fell slowly in a long deep-drawn sigh.

"Why speakest thou in tone so melancholy?" I asked. "Thou hast youth, health, long life, everything before thee!"

"No," she answered gravely, with her white pointed chin still resting thoughtfully upon her palm. "Already I am threatened; nay, I am doomed."

"How?" I enquired, incredulously.

"Listen, and I will explain," she said, slowly, raising her beautiful eyes to mine. "About two moons ago, attired in the *haick* of an Arab woman, I journeyed with my aged uncle to In Salah, in order to make purchases in the market, as is our custom twice each year. On our return hither we came across an encampment of those red-legged dogs of French, and having accepted the hospitality of their tents through several days on account of the sand-storms, I was surprised and annoyed by receiving a declaration of love from the young lieutenant in charge, whose name was Victor Gaillard, and whose home, he told me, was in

Paris. Believing me to be daughter of an Arab merchant, he announced his readiness to take me to Algiers and make me his wife; but hating these youthful irresponsible masters of our land, I declined that honour. He then declared that at all costs I should be his, for at the end of the year he was going north to the seashore, where he would be quartered until the spring, and that if I escaped him he and his host who ruled the Desert would treat me and my people as rebellious, and shoot us down like dogs. I laughed his declaration to scorn, for he little dreamed of my real name, birth, and dwelling-place. Next day I remained in the encampment, but on the following night, by bribing one of the Spahi sentries with a ring from my finger, I and my uncle managed to escape, and, beneath the crescent moon, pushed our way forward in the direction of Saba. Through four days we travelled almost incessantly, until at midnight on the fifth our camels' feet sank deep into the quicksands that render the entrance to Saba unapproachable. Laughing as I congratulated myself on my cleverness at outwitting him, I had gone some hundred paces when, chancing to glance back, I saw not far away, hesitating at the edge of the treacherous belt of ground, a single horseman. The glint of moonlight on his bright scabbard showed him to be an officer of the Roumis, and instantly I recognised the slim silhouette of Victor Gaillard. He sat motionless in his saddle, and with his field-glass raised calmly watched our difficult progress towards the two colossal statues which have guarded the entrance to our city from the day of King Solomon. My uncle, noticing my alarm, also turned and detected our pursuer. That night, before my family assembled in the palace, I explained the whole of the facts, and they, knowing how relentless are these harsh infidel rulers of ours, unanimously decided upon flight. But I declined to leave. Was I not Balkîs, Queen of Saba? Was not the great store of gold and jewels given into my keeping that I should remain and watch them until I drew my last breath? They urged me to accompany them into the mountains, but finding me obdurate all fled, leaving me alone to face the unscrupulous man who had declared that at all costs I should become his wife. Ten weary anxious days have since gone by. Yesterday thou earnest hither, thy face wrapped in thy black *litham*, and naturally I supposed thou wert the accursed infidel in disguise. I watched thee explore my palace and enter to the cave wherein my treasure lieth concealed. When thou hadst entered I breathed more freely, full well knowing that thou hadst gone forward into thy grave."

"How? Is the tunnel azotic?"

"No. Within is an ingenious mechanical contrivance which was constructed by Balkîs herself, whereby the unsuspecting intruder releases a spring, and is struck down by a great iron mace."

"I was struck," I observed.

She nodded, smiling sadly.

"When I went forward to ascertain whether mine enemy still lived I found thy veil unloosened, and that thy features were not those of the hateful Frank. Then I tended thee throughout the night, and at dawn thou didst rally and art now rapidly recovering."

"Of a verity I had a narrow escape."

"Assuredly thou didst. Many others, as adventurous and stout-hearted as thyself, have met their fate at that spot."

"So thou hast remained here alone and single-handed to guard the treasure of thine ancestor against the pilfering of the Franks?" I said, regarding the beautiful, frail-looking girl with admiration. "Assuredly thou art as courageous as the great Balkîs who defied the combined powers of the ancient world."

She sighed. "It hath been the duty of the Queens of Saba to remain within their kingdom even if evil threatened and all forsake them. I will never be wife of a Frank, neither will I exhibit fear to these new rulers of the Desert who are led by amorous youths from Paris boulevards," she answered, drawing herself up with queenly hauteur.

"Peradventure he only useth idle threats," I observed.

"No. The Franks who conquered Algeria and hold it beneath the thraldom of the religion they call Christianity, are our rulers also. He ordered me to remain in the encampment on pain of being outlawed. I disobeyed; therefore I and my people are rebels. That he will return and seek me out I am convinced."

"Then why not fly?" I suggested. "I will take thee to where my tribe, are encamped. Although we are thieves and brigands, thou, a woman, wilt nevertheless meet with chivalrous treatment at our hands."

She shook her head, and with dogged persistence announced her intention of remaining, while, on my part, I promised to render her whatever assistance lay in my power.

"Then first help me to remove the throne into the treasure-house," she said, and opening a door that had been concealed behind the heavy hangings she led me into the great hall where water flowed beneath its pavement of glass.

Together we dragged the bejewelled seat of royalty through several courts, until we came to the small pavilion which gave entrance to the cavern. Then, while she carried a flaming flambeau, I toiled on with it after her. When we had gone some distance into the heart of the mountain she stooped to secure the ancient mechanism so that the iron mace could not again descend, and advancing some further distance we found ourselves in a kind of *cul-de-sac*, with only a black wall of rock before us. To the right, however, was a cunningly-concealed door which gave entrance to a spacious natural chamber, wherein I saw, heaped indiscriminately, the most wondrous collection of golden ornaments and brilliant jewels my eyes had ever gazed upon. Some of them I took up, holding them in my hand in wonderment. The gems were of the first water, the spoils taken in battle by the notorious queen once feared by all the world, while heaped everywhere were bejewelled breast-plates, gem-encrusted goblets, golden dishes, and swords with hilts and scabbards thickly set with precious stones. Wheresoever I trod there were scattered in the fine white dust strings of pearls, uncut gems, rings, and ear-ornaments, while all around were piled great immovable boxes of hewn stone, like coffins, securely clamped with rusting iron. These had never been opened, and contained, according to the story of my companion, the tribute of enormous worth sent by King Solomon to Balkîs. These I examined carefully, one after another, at length discovering one, the stone of which had split so that a small aperture was formed. I placed my hand inside and withdrew it, holding between my thumb and finger three cut diamonds, the like of which I had never before beheld. The stone box was filled to the brim with gems of every kind.

In wonderment I was standing, contemplating this vast wealth of a vanished nation, when my fair conductress exclaimed—

"There is still one other marvel about this place. Listen! Canst thou hear a sound?"

Distinctly I heard a dull, monotonous boom, which had continued uninterruptedly ever since we had been there.

"Yea. What is its cause?" I asked.

"The interior of this mountain is as a fiery furnace. That roaring is the unquenchable flame that has burned therein through ages. During mine own remembrance as a child smoke hath issued from the cone above, and so near are we to the fiery interior here in this treasure-house that its very walls are warm."

Upon the rock I placed my hand, and so hot was it that I was compelled to withdraw it instantly. Only a thin partition of stone apparently divided us from the mysterious fathomless crater.

"One of the beliefs that have come down unto me through ages," Balkîs said, "is that within this place is Al-Hâwiyat, the dwelling prepared for infidels and pagans, where their food shall be offal, and they shall slake their thirst with boiling pitch."

"Allah is mighty and wise," I answered. "Alone he knoweth the hearts of his servants. May perfect peace remain ever upon thee."

"And upon thee, O Ahamadou," she responded, raising her bright eyes earnestly to mine. "Now that I have shown thee this, the wealth of my ancestors, thou wilt promise never to conspire to gain possession of it while any of my family remain here in Saba."

"Although of a tribe of thieves, I swear by Allah's might that never will I expose thy secret, nor will I seek to possess myself of what is thine," I answered. "Thy family shall ever be as mine, for I am no abuser of the salt."

"In thee do I place my trust," she answered, allowing her soft hand, the hand that had so deftly bandaged my injured brow and bathed my face—to linger for an instant within my grasp.

Then, drawing from my pouch the great lustrous ruby I had stolen, I handed it back to her. But she made me retain it as *souvenir* of my visit to Saba, the city forgotten.

The atmosphere in the treasure-house was stifling. Having, therefore, deposited the throne of Balkîs in fitting place, we left, returning through the concealed door to the narrow burrow which had exit in the small pavilion. Side by side we slowly crossed court after court of the great palace which had witnessed pageants of such magnificence that their splendour has been proverbial till this day, she pointing out the principal objects of interest, halting to explain curious sculptured wall-pictures and inscriptions commemorating the triumphs of the great queen, or pausing to recall some long-forgotten story of love, hatred, or malice connected with the spot whereon we stood. In that mellow sunset-hour, as we lingered together beneath the cool shadows, I learnt more of the historic, time-effaced empire of Balkîs than savants have ever known. As scholar, it delighted me to hear it from the lips of one who had descended in the direct royal line from that famous woman, who, according to our Sura, entitled "The Ant," became convinced during her visit to Solomon that, by worshipping the sun she had dealt unjustly with her own soul, and resigned herself unto Allah, the lord of all creatures.

She had given me some wine and dates, and we had passed through the great hall with its transparent pavement and out upon the terrace before the palace when, of a sudden, a loud cry escaped her.

"See!" she gasped, dismayed. "See! The Franks are here!"

Next second a hulking Zouave who had secreted himself behind one of the great sculptured columns sprang upon her. She uttered a loud scream; but, ere he could secure her hands, I had drawn my poignard and dealt him an unerring blow, causing him to reel and fall back heavily upon the stones.

A dozen soldiers, headed by Victor Gaillard, their evil-faced, narrow-browed, moustached officer in his gold-laced uniform and cherry-coloured trousers, had nearly gained the top of the steps. But the ugly sight of blood had already unnerved my fair companion, who, turning quickly to me, cried—

"Let us fly! Follow me. There is but one way to escape."

She rushed away, and I followed, our pursuers close at our heels. I no longer wore my black *litham*, therefore the elegant youth from Paris, sent by the French to rule the Dwellers of the Desert, could not have been aware that I was a Touareg, one of the bandits of the Azjar, whom he amused himself by hunting when inclined for sport. Onward we sped, crossing court after court, until we again entered the subterranean burrow, and groping along it in the darkness, my companion found at last another secret door, which she opened, pushed me into it, and entering herself, closed it. Then we listened. There was no sound. Apparently our pursuers had not dared to follow us there.

"This," she explained beneath her breath, "leadeth by a secret way out upon the mountain-side. We may yet escape."

Upward we toiled in a tunnel so narrow that ofttimes we were compelled to crawl upon hands and knees, yet ever ascending, and feeling our way, we at last, after half an hour's frantic effort, saw a faint glimmer of light above, and succeeded in emerging upon the bare rocky side of the giant mountain.

"Let us mount still higher and pass along to the other side," she urged. "I know the path."

Together we started off in the fast falling gloom, when suddenly I heard an exclamation in French, and, looking down, saw Gaillard, with three of his Zouaves below us, scrambling up as quickly as they were able.

Instantly I saw that their further progress was barred by a sheer cliff of rock quite fifty feet in height, and that we were in a position impregnable. Balkîs, noticing our situation, also turned towards him with a low scornful laugh.

Next instant the fierce uncurbed anger of this young *boulevardier* found vent, for, with a loud imprecation in French he declared that she should never escape him, and ere I could divine his intention he had snatched a rifle from the man standing at his side and covered the woman he had desired to marry.

I sprang quickly towards my fellow-fugitive; but ere I could drag her down to earth, our only cover, there was a flash, a loud report, and Balkîs, with a shrill shriek, stumbled forward mortally wounded, and rolling helplessly down the mountain-side, fell dead almost at the very feet of her brutal murderer.

The gold-braided officer laughed.

It was one of the most heartless assassinations I had ever witnessed, but knowing that efforts would undoubtedly be made to shoot me also, I threw myself upon my stomach and crawled upward quickly with hands and toes.

"See, men; I have brought down the dainty little bird!" I heard Gaillard exclaim, as he walked to where the body was lying crumpled in a heap. "Give me her necklaces and bracelets. The rest of her jewels you may divide. She was merely a rebel. It is our duty to repress revolt, even though we may sometimes be compelled to shoot women."

The Zouaves ruthlessly tore the jewels from the body of the last remaining daughter of the Queen of Saba, while their lieutenant amused himself by firing at me. A dozen shots he sent after me, but all the bullets sang over my head, until at last, when the darkness became complete, I halted, breathless, behind a projection of rock, and there waited, watching from my elevated position the camp fires lighted, and the soldiers exploring the deserted ruins by the aid of flambeaux.

Once during the night I thought I heard a noise like thunder, and distinctly felt the mountain tremble. But soon after dawn I had the satisfaction of seeing our enemies strike their camp and march slowly out towards the plain. The few jewels they found about the palace they had divided among themselves, and were apparently in high glee.

Having remained in hiding three hours after their departure I descended, passing the body of the hapless Balkîs, already surrounded by a screaming crowd of grey vultures, and, re-entering the palace to ascertain the extent of the depredations of the Franks, I was amazed to discover a dense black smoke issuing from the pavilion before the mouth of the cave. I tried to advance, but sulphurous fumes almost overcame me. Instantly I discerned the truth. The thin partition of rock which divided the treasure-house from the burning crater within had been broken through, and the suppressed fire of the volcano was issuing in great volume from the burrow, together with quantities of molten lava and ashes which have since entirely overwhelmed the ruins.

Three years afterwards I had occasion to travel to Algiers to see Gaillard, then raised to a responsible position in the Bureau Arabe, regarding a Zouave whom we had captured and afterwards set free. I casually mentioned the buried ruins of the forgotten City of the Seven Shadows at the spot he knew so well, but he merely replied—

"Ah! yes, I know. I once explored them and found a curious cave there in the side of the mountain. I blew it up with dynamite in order that it should not be used as a hiding-place by any of your veiled tribe. The explosion, however, much to our dismay, opened a suppressed volcano, with the result that fire issued forth, killing all six of our men who performed the work."

Victor Gaillard, although now a Colonel, and back in his beloved Paris, where he sits in the Chamber of Deputies as representative of a constituency in the Alpes Maritimes, does not know that by the irresponsible use of his explosive he lost for ever the greatest collection of gold and jewels that has ever been brought together.

The only single gem of the vast treasure of Balkîs that has been preserved is the magnificent blood-red ruby which at this moment adorns my sword-hilt. In both colour and size it is matchless. Never can I handle that weapon without reflecting upon its tragic story, or without visions rising to my eyes of the beautiful queen who reigned so briefly over her vanished and forgotten kingdom.

Chapter Two.

A Sappho of the Sand.

Throughout our breathless land of sun and silence there is a well-known adage that the word of a Veiled Man is like water poured upon sand which, when once dropped, is never to be recovered. I am, alas, compelled to admit that there is much truth in this; nevertheless, to every rule there is an exception, and in every tribe of the Touaregs, from those of the Tidikelt to those of the Adrar, are to be found men who are not thieves or evil-doers, even though they may be marauders.

Those acquainted with the progress of recent events in Algeria will remember that when our brothers, the Kabyles, rose against our now masters, the French, and committed the terrible massacres at Al-Setit, news was promptly circulated over every one of the vast Saharan plains that the forces of Al-Islâm had, at last, risen against the infidels. Eager for the fray, most of the desert tribes, among them the Touaregs of the Benin Sissin, Haratin, and Kel-Owi, or "People of the Light," united against the Roumis. Hence, we of the Azjar pressed northward in force in order to unite with the warlike Beni-Mzab in a formidable attack upon the French posts at Gardaia and Wargla, south of the great Atlas range. Assembling at the El Gettara oasis we left our women, old men, and children encamped, crossed the high sunbaked lands of the Tademayt, then, passing up the rocky waterless valley of the Miya, traversed the region of bare red sand-hills known as the Erg, and leaving Wargla fifty miles to the east, set our camels' heads towards Metlili, halting one day's march off that town.

In ordinary circumstances we should never have dared to approach so near the sphere of French influence, especially as this was the region of the Beni-Mzabs, who zealously guarded any encroachment upon their territory. But war had been declared against the infidel, and the Shorfa (Faithful) were uniting beneath the green banner of Al-Islâm. At high noon we halted, and soon afterwards there appeared a French Colonel with a large escort of his scarlet-burnoused Spahis. The officer, who had ridden from Metlili to intercept us, was received courteously by Tamahu, our Sheikh. He demanded the payment of taxes, but the proud old man whom I have since succeeded answered, "Tell that lord of yours, that if he wants our taxes he can come for them himself, and we will make sure he gets them, in silver coins too, for we will roll each franc into a bullet, and deliver it to him ourselves." The Colonel declared that the taxes must be paid, but our Sheikh courteously requested the infidel and his horsemen to return to the town.

"Then you intend fighting?" the Colonel asked, at last.

"We do," answered Tamahu. "Tell thy lord that The Breath of the Wind decline to make submission to the French."

"You intend attacking Metlili?" the officer enquired, thoughtfully, twirling his pointed moustache.

Our Sheikh nodded, his keen eyes watching the face of the infidel. The latter's countenance grew grave, whereat we, standing around leaning on our spears, laughed in derision.

"Thou art of the great army of the infidels," Tamahu said. "Yet thy face palest when we speak of conflict!"

The officer started, and knit his grey brows.

"I fear not thine host of Veiled Men, fierce and relentless though ye be. True, I am a soldier, but one thing alone I dread."

"Thou fearest to lose thy life," observed our Sheikh, knowing that the garrison at that little desert town was but small and weak.

"For myself I care nothing," the Colonel answered. "It is the fate of my daughter that I fear."

"Thy daughter! Why is she here, in the desert, so far from Algiers?"

"Not having seen me for four years she travelled from Paris a moon ago to visit me. Both my captain and my lieutenant have died of fever, and we two are now the only Europeans in Metlili. The rising of thy tribesmen hath occurred so unexpectedly, or I would have sent her under escort back to the coast."

"Is thy daughter a child?" asked Tamahu.

"She is nineteen," answered the officer, whose name he informed us was Colonel Bonnemain. We at once knew him by repute as a distinguished traveller and soldier.

"Thou knowest what is said of the word of a Touareg," the Sheikh said, regarding him keenly.

The Colonel nodded.

"Canst thou trust these my tribesmen with the escort of thy daughter?" Tamahu asked. "If thou wilt, no harm shall befall her. We have agreed with the Mzabs to attack and pillage thy town, because thou, with thine horsemen, hast established a post therein; therefore it must be done. But the Azjars wage not war upon women, and ere we commence the attack thy daughter shall find safe asylum within our camp."

For a moment the Colonel hesitated, looking intently into the dark, bright eyes of our aged headman. But seeing honesty and truth mirrored in his face the infidel held out his hand, and in silence more eloquent than words gripped that of his enemy. At last his tongue's strings became loosened.

"Henceforth, although I am an officer of the French, and compelled to fight against thee, I am nevertheless thy friend, and some day will prove my friendship. Gabrielle shall be within thy camp at dawn."

"The Azjars will give her the welcome of friends," answered our Sheikh.

With a brief expression of heartfelt thanks Colonel Bonnemain vaulted lightly into his saddle, and wishing us "Peace," spurred away to where his troop of expectant Spahis awaited him.

"May Allah guard thee and thine!" answered Tamahu in response to the infidel's salutation, and a moment later our enemies were riding hard away towards the far-off horizon.

The long breathless afternoon went slowly by. We had not encamped, because we knew not when our allies, the Beni-Mzabs, might approach, and rapidity of movement was of urgent necessity, inasmuch as a formidable French column was on the march. Spent by long travel, the majority of us stretched ourselves on the hot sands and slept, leaving half-a-dozen to act as sentinels and prevent surprise; but at the *maghrib* hour all were awakened by the clear voice of our aged marabout reciting the *fâtihat*. Every man, without exception, knelt upon the sand, his back turned upon the blaze of crimson in the west, and recited the *suras*, praying to Allah to prosper our expedition.

When we arose, Tamahu, his right hand raised to heaven, and his left grasping his gleaming spear, exhorted us to remain faithful, and to bear arms bravely against the infidels.

"Ye are called forth against a mighty and a warlike nation," he exclaimed. "Ye shall fight against them, or they shall profess Islam. If ye obey, Allah will, of a verity, give you a glorious reward; but if ye turn back he will chastise you with a grievous chastisement. Allah has promised you many spoils, which ye should take; and he giveth these by way of earnest; and he restraineth the hand of man from you; and the same may be a sign unto the true believers; and he guideth you in the right way. Allah knoweth that which ye know not; and he hath appointed you, besides this, a speedy victory."

Long and earnestly the old Sheikh addressed us, quoting from our Book of Everlasting Will to emphasise his declarations. Then he referred to the compact he had that day made with the leader of our enemies.

"A woman of the Franks we shall receive into this our camp. Remember, O my people, that she will partake of our salt, and that while this war continueth she is our friend. Let not a single hair of her head be injured. The word of thy Sheikh Tamahu hath already been given."

That evening we spent in sharpening our spears and shangermangors, preparatory to the fight, singing snatches of war-songs and discussing the prospects of the attack. Perhaps of all the tribes in the trackless solitudes which constitute our home, we of the Azjar are among the most active, vigorous, and enterprising, inured as we are to hardships, and with our mental faculties sharpened almost to a preternatural degree by the hard struggle for existence in our arid rocky fastnesses. The rearing of oxen, horses, and goats is our chief occupation, but the scarcity of water and our speedy exhaustion of the scanty pasturage of the oases keep us perpetually on the march. Agriculture is scarcely possible under a sky from which rain does not fall for six or eight consecutive years; therefore it is, perhaps, not surprising that we have developed into desert-pirates.

Those who have never set foot upon the Saharan plains can possess but a vague idea of their appearance. In the whole of the Great Desert, a track comprising over two million square miles, there is not a single carriage-road, not a mile of navigable waters, not a wheeled vehicle, canoe, or boat of any kind. There are scarcely even any beaten tracks, for most of the routes, though followed for ages without divergence of any kind, are temporarily effaced by every sandstorm, and recovered only by means of the permanent landmarks—wells, prominent dunes, a solitary eminence crowned with a solitary bush, the remains of travellers, slaves, or camels that may have perished of thirst or exhaustion between the stations.

Long and patiently we waited for the arrival of the woman to whom we had promised protection; but although the night passed, the dawn rose, and the hours crept on towards the noon, our vigilance remained unrewarded. A second day passed in inactivity, then, wearied of waiting, we struck camp and moved forward.

The afterglow had deepened into evening dusk when at length we came within sight of Metlili. Looming high up on a pinnacle of rock, white against the clear sky, its appearance astonished us, for it looked impregnable. Its flat-roofed houses rose tier upon tier around an exceedingly steep eminence crowned by a great mosque with high square minaret, while at the foot of the hill were some scattered date-groves.

We had passed over the summit of a sand ridge, and were making a dash straight upon the French stronghold, when we noticed that our presence had already been detected. Upon the walls a few Spahis in scarlet and some white-burnoused Arabs were moving hurriedly. Suddenly there was a flash from the Kasbah, followed by a report, loud, sharp, echoless. Our enemies had opened fire upon us.

Tamahu instantly gave the word to spur forward on the wings of haste. With one accord we rode in a huge compact body so swiftly as to justify our popular appellation "The Breath of the Wind," and, regardless of a rapid rifle-fire that was poured out from the white walls, pressed forward to the foot of the rock. Here we dismounted, and with loud yells of savage rage dashed up the rough narrow way that gave entrance to the town. Many of my companions fell dead or wounded ere they reached the hastily-barred gate, but by dint of fierce and dogged determination, we pushed forward in force so great that we managed to at last batter down the huge wooden doors. Next second we poured into the place in overwhelming numbers. Up its steep streets, so narrow that two asses could not pass abreast, we engaged Spahis and Zouaves hand-to-hand. So strong was our force that soon we overwhelmed them, and commenced loud cries of triumph as we dashed up towards the Kasbah. Suddenly, however, as we approached it we saw that its walls literally swarmed with French soldiers who, at word of command, fired a withering volley from their rifles which caused us to hold back dismayed.

Colonel Bonnemain had evidently received reinforcements. With their firearms they were more than a match for us.

"Courage, brothers!" I heard Tamahu cry as he brandished his spear. "Let us show these dogs of infidels that the Touaregs are no cowards. Of a verity the Roumis shall never be our masters."

With set teeth we sprang forward towards the high sun-blanched walls of the citadel, determined to take it by assault, but alas! its battlements were full of well-armed Spahis and Turcos, and from every point showers of lead swept down upon us. Still we kept on undaunted. Once I caught a momentary glimpse of Colonel Bonnemain. He was standing upon the wall bareheaded, shouting and waving his sword. But only for an instant. He disappeared, and was seen no more.

Almost at the same instant a loud incessant spitting of guns deafened us; bullets swept through our ranks in deadly hail, killing us by dozens and maiming hundreds. Then, dismayed, I saw mounted on the wall a strange-looking weapon, which once charged shed rifle-balls in hundreds. Death seemed inevitable. My companions, appalled by the sight of that terrible engine of destruction, wavered for an instant, then, with a cry that Eblis was assisting the infidels, turned and fled.

Above the din of battle Tamahu shouted himself hoarse. But darkness having now fallen, none could discern him amid the dense smoke and constant flashing of the guns. Thus the defenders drove us back, sweeping us away with their deadly machine-gun, and, making a sortie from the fortress, bayonetted the more valiant ones.

Our cause seemed lost. As soon, however, as we had drawn the Spahis outside their fort, we turned, and re-engaging them hand-to-hand, quickly hacked our way back to the very gates of the Kasbah, the streets in the vicinity being heaped with dead and dying. Suddenly, however, at the moment when we were relinquishing our hope as a forlorn one, loud shouts, followed by the beating of tam-tams, gave us renewed courage. From mouth to mouth the glad tidings were repeated. The Beni-Mzabs, one of the most powerful tribes on the desert border, had come up, and being our allies, were rendering us assistance.

Of the exciting moments which immediately succeeded, I have but vague remembrance. Suffice it to say that the warlike race of the Atlas to the number of two thousand poured into Metlili, and with our forces combined we succeeded in dislodging and totally annihilating the French garrison. Everywhere throughout the town fighting quickly became general, but in such numbers had we now assembled that those holding the Kasbah were compelled to sue for peace. The Beni-Mzabs declined, however, to give quarter, consequently the scenes of bloodshed were terrible to behold. Before dawn the sack of the town had commenced, and everywhere the firebrand was applied. The loot obtainable was, we found, of very little value, nevertheless both the Beni-Mzabs and our own tribesmen were in high glee at their first success against the infidel forces. It was regarded as precursory of a great victory.

Just as the sun was rising I was inside the ancient citadel so recently the infidel stronghold, and was exploring its many courts with their old blue-tiled fountains and cool, handsome colonnades, when suddenly as I passed beneath an archway in the thickness of the wall a noise startled me. My companions in arms were regaling themselves in an open square before the great white mosque, therefore I was alone. Around me lay many bodies of Touaregs, Spahis, and Beni-Mzabs, while some of the wounded were still groaning, dying slowly, for there had been no attempt to succour the disabled. To fall in a holy war is not a misfortune, but the reverse. The noise, a loud knock, again sounded, and turning I saw a bolted door, which I at once opened, and was confronted by a pretty dark-haired French girl, who, glancing at me in terror for an instant, screamed and fled down a flight of stone stairs into an impenetrable darkness.

In a moment I dashed after her. Already the Kasbah had been set on fire, and to save her life instant escape was necessary. Below, in the small foul stone chamber, used long ago as a prison, I discovered her crouching. She screamed loudly at my approach, fearing me, perhaps, because of the mysterious black veil across my face, and knowing that the Veiled Men were of evil repute.

"Thou art Mademoiselle Gabrielle, daughter of our friend Colonel Bonnemain," I exclaimed in the best French I could articulate. "Fear not, but fly at once with me, or we may both lose our lives."

"How knowest thou my name?" she gasped in amazement. By the glimmer of light that came from the open court above I saw that her face was beautiful but deathly pale. "True, I am daughter of Colonel Bonnemain, but thou art a Touareg. Assuredly thou art our enemy, not our friend. Why, it was thine hosts who attacked us!"

Briefly I explained the promise of our Sheikh, assuring her of our friendship. At first she was inclined to doubt my sincerity, but at length I prevailed upon her to accompany me in our race for life from the burning ruins. Quickly we sought Tamahu, and as there were no women with us she was at once placed under my protection. I was to be her guardian and her champion during the remainder of hostilities. Long and earnestly we both searched and enquired for her father, the Colonel, but could discover no trace of him. Some of his Spahis who survived declared that he had been struck down in the earlier hours of the conflict, while others maintained that they had seen him fighting uninjured up to the very last. From our enquiries it appeared evident that, on receiving unexpected reinforcements from the north, he had determined upon holding out against us, and overlooking our agreement with the Beni-Mzabs, was ill-advised enough to decline our good offices. Then, when he found an attack in force being made, he locked Gabrielle in a place of safety until the fight should end.

Full of excitement were those days that followed. I must, however, here confess that within twenty-four hours I found myself deeply attached to this bright-eyed fragile girl whoso gallant father had disappeared so mysteriously. We, of the Azjars, leaving the prosperous town of Metlili a mere pile of smoking ruins, encamped for a few days in the vicinity where there was an excellent well, then together with the fierce horsemen of the Beni-Mzab set our heads towards Wargla, another French outpost. At first Gabrielle felt the fatigue of travel terribly. Fortunately she could ride well, and as her inseparable companion, I endeavoured to render her journey as comfortable as possible. At my suggestion she had exchanged her European clothes for the *serroual* and *haick* of the Arab women, finding that mode of dress more comfortable and less conspicuous than her own; and so light-hearted she grew that not unfrequently she would join me in a cigarette. Her grace and manner charmed us all. The fierce horsemen of the Azjar and the Beni-Mzab are scarcely chivalrous where women are concerned, but ere we had been on the march three days there was not a single tribesman who would not execute her slightest wish.

Riding day by day over the breathless solitudes of sand, no single word of complaint ever escaped her. Whenever we halted, before she ate she would busy herself in attending to our wounded; sometimes bandaging an arm or a leg, at others pouring out water and handing it to a thirsty man with a pleasing smile that quickened his pulse. Then, after we had eaten and turned our faces to the Holy Ca'aba, she would take an old Spanish mandoline which one of my companions had picked up cheap long ago in Oran, and play and sing to us in a sweet contralto songs from her own far-off Paris. They were mostly gay *chansons*, such as one hears in the *cafés* in Algiers, and those with refrains were sung lustily in chorus by the whole of the great assembly.

One night after she had given us several songs I persuaded her to dance. To those unaccustomed to life in the desert the scene would have appeared a strange one. The bright moonlight shining full upon her, tipped also with silver the keen heads of a couple of thousand spears upon which her audience leaned. She had fascinated them. Unanimously it had been declared that she was an enchantress. Only one fact remained to mar her happiness: her uncertainty regarding her father's fate.

"I will dance on one condition, Ahamadou," she answered in French, throwing back her pretty head and showing her white teeth as she laughed.

"What is that?"

"I will dance if thou wilt take off that hideous black veil. Thou hast been my friend all this time, yet, strangely enough, I have never beheld thy face."

I hesitated. Such a demand was unusual, for a Touareg never removes his veil.

My companions overhearing, and noticing my disinclination to acquiesce, with one accord urged me to accede, and at last, amid much good humour, I unwound my black *litham*.

Long and earnestly she looked into my eyes. Her gaze lingered upon me strangely, I thought; then suddenly clapping her hands, she raised her long white arms above her head, and to the thumping of four *derboukas*, one of which I held, she commenced a slow graceful dance. Never tired of exerting herself to comfort the wounded or amuse those who were her father's bitterest foes, she danced on until she sank completely out of breath. Then she reclined upon the soft rugs spread for her, and, with Tamahu and myself, smoked a cigarette in silence. From her full red lips she blew clouds of smoke, and watched it curl upward in the still night air. I glanced at her furtively, and saw that she had grown unusually thoughtful. Her brilliant eyes were fixed upon the stars.

At last, pillowing her handsome head upon a leopard's skin I rolled and placed for her, she wished me "Peace," and presently closed her eyes in sleep.

Silence, dead and complete, had fallen upon the camp. The stillness was only broken by the uneasy groaning of a camel or the soft footfall of a sentry whose spear gleamed afar in the white moonbeams. Gabrielle's heart slowly heaved and fell as she slept. Through that calm night I sat, hugging my knees and thinking deeply. Try how I would, I could not get rid of the one thought that for days had possessed me, the thought of her. That she had entranced me; that she held me in her toils irrevocably, I could not deny. Never before had I looked upon any woman with affection until now. But I loved with all my heart and soul this delicate Roumi, whose fair face the sun had never kissed.

Was it not in order to behold my countenance she had that evening requested me to remove my *litham*? Her every word, her every action, now that I recalled them, showed plainly that she did not regard me with disfavour. The moon waned, the stars paled, and dawn was nigh ere I cast myself upon the warm sand near her, and snatched a brief hour's repose, not, however, before I had carefully placed a rug about her, fearing lest the morning dew, so deadly to Europeans, should chill her.

One bright balmy night we reached El Okaz, and halted. It was a large oasis with running water, luxuriant vegetation, and many palms. When the *maghrib* had been said, the evening meal eaten, and the sun was slowly sinking, I went forth among the trees to search for camel-grass, and invited Gabrielle to accompany me. She walked by my side, and when we were out of hearing I took her tiny hand in mine, and, raising it reverently to my lips, declared my love.

Slowly, but resolutely, she drew her hand away. The last ray of sunlight tipped her hair with molten gold as we stood together beneath a great high palm. Her brilliant eyes glistened with unshed tears.

"Alas! no, Ahamadou," she answered huskily. "We must not love each other, it would wreck both our lives."

"Why not?" I cried passionately, my arm around her waist, her slim white hand raised again to my lips. "I adore you. To me thou art my life, my love, my everything."

"Ah! yes," she sighed sadly. "To you I owe my life. You have all been so good to me, although I am a woman of the Franks, that I can scarce believe that you are actually the Azjars, the dreaded Breath of the Wind, reports of whose exploits have times without number caused me to shudder."

"An Azjar never forgets a favour nor forgives a false friend," I answered. "To our enemies we are brutal and relentless; yet those who eat our salt need never fear. Already hast thou had experience of the treatment the stranger receiveth within our tents."

"True," she answered, her hand closing tightly over mine. "I have had experience of thine own tender care of me, Ahamadou, yet—"

"Yet thou hast already grown tired of our life?" I hazarded reproachfully.

"Ah! no," she said quickly, fixing her brilliant eyes upon mine. "Thou hast asked if I could ever love thee. I tell thee that I do love thee, yet there is between us a barrier of blood, and such love can only bring unhappiness unto us both."

"Thou lovest me!" I cried, delighted, and taking her soft cheeks between my hard, sun-browned hands, our lips met for the first time in a long passionate caress. Again, she put me from her, saying—"No, it can never be. We are of different races, different creeds. What is right in thine eyes is sin in mine; what is worship to thee is, to me, idolatry. No, Ahamadou. It must not be. We must not love, for we can never marry."

I was silent. Her argument seemed utterly unassailable. Never before had I faced the situation until now. She had, indeed, spoken the truth.

"But we love each other!" I cried, dolefully.

"Yes," she sighed, shaking her head. "I confess that I love thee," and her fingers again gripped my hand. "But it is the very fact that we love one another that should cause us to part and forget."

"Why? Until the war is ended thou must, of necessity, remain in our camp," I observed.

"And after?"

"Then we could return to Algiers, or to Oran, and marry."

She remained silent for a few moments, nervously toying with the single ring of emeralds upon her finger.

"No," she answered at length. "This love between us is but a passing fancy. When the war is at an end, thou wilt have become convinced of the truth of my words."

"Never," I answered. "I love thee now; I shall love thee always."

"Alas!" she said, laying her hand softly upon my shoulder, and looking earnestly into my face. "Now that we have both made confession we must endeavour to forget. We love each other, but the wide difference in our races renders happiness impossible. Thou wilt find for wife some good woman of thine own people, and I—perhaps I shall find some man of mine own nationality to become my husband. From to-night, Ahamadou, if thou lovest me, thou wilt make no further sign."

I bit my lip to the blood. Although she had uttered these words, I saw that she nevertheless loved me with a mad, passionate love, for soon down her pink cheeks tears were coursing.

"Thou art all to me—everything, Gabrielle," I cried. "Allah knoweth how deeply and honestly I adore thee, I—"

The sound of a rifle-shot startled us. With bated breath we both strained our ears. The evening gloom had crept on unperceived, and it was almost dark. In rapid succession other shots sounded, followed by the fierce fiendish war-cry of the Beni-Mzabs. Instantly the truth flashed upon me. We had been surprised by the French!

By the route we had come we sped back to the encampment, where we found all confusion. A large body of Spahis had made a sudden and determined attack, but it had been repulsed. My first thought was of Gabrielle's safety. I found cover for her behind a huge boulder, and telling her to seat herself, and not attempt to watch the progress of the fight, returned, spear in hand, to bear my part against our enemies.

The cessation of the fighting was only for a few minutes. We heard the sudden sound of a bugle, and from among the trees there dashed a formidable troop of red-burnoused horsemen, led by a young European officer, who sat his horse as if he were part of it. Even in that moment of excitement I admired the way he rode. The charge was, however, an ill-fated one. Not half those who dashed forward lived to retreat. The Arabs of the Mechefer, who had recently joined us, possessed guns, and the flashing of these, in combination with those of our enemies, illumined the darkness, while the still air was full of dense, stifling smoke. More desperate each moment the conflict grew. Undismayed by loss or misfortune, we thrice returned their attack, each time with increasing force, until our bullets and keen spears commenced to work havoc among the infidel ranks. East and furious became the fight, but gradually the attack upon us grew weaker, and at last, determined upon reprisals, Tamahu ordered a dash forward. With one accord we charged, and then before us the remnant of the ill-fated troop fell back and fled to save their lives.

When I returned I found Gabrielle kneeling beside the officer whose riding had been so conspicuous, tenderly bandaging an ugly spear-wound he had received in the left shoulder. She had improvised a torch, and beneath its fitful light was pursuing her task unconscious of my approach. Upon the clammy brow of the unconscious man she placed her cool, soft hand; then, having felt his pulse, she seemed satisfied, and taking her flambeau went forward to one of my own tribesmen who had been injured in the breast. From the deep shadow wherein I stood I watched her, white-robed and fair like one of the good genii of whom the Korân tells us, passing from one to another, alleviating their sufferings as best she could, uttering cheering words, or giving water to the dying. I did not approach her, for my heart seemed too full. It was best, I thought, to leave her alone to her merciful work.

Before the sun rose many of those whom she had so carefully tended and watched had drawn their last breath, but the young officer, whose name I afterwards learned was André de Freyville, lieutenant of Spahis, had recovered consciousness sufficiently to thank his nurse, and learn from her lips the curious circumstances which had led her to accept the hospitality of our tents. He proved a pleasant fellow, and during his convalescence we all three had frequent chats together. Although he was our prisoner-of-war, he soon became on excellent terms with Tamahu, and his time passed happily enough. Colonel Bonnemain had, he told us, escaped when Metlili fell, and had reached Algiers unharmed.

Soon, in order to join forces with another large body of horsemen moving from the great Hammada, or stony tableland, in Tripoli, we advanced to the oasis of Medagin, two days' march from El Aghouat, then held in such force by the French that we dared not attack it.

Reaching Medagin at noon, we encamped. When the stars shone both Gabrielle and De Freyville sang us some French *chansons*, the one accompanying the other upon the mandoline. Before we scooped out our hollows in the sand to form our couches I borrowed a gun from one of the Arabs, intending to go out at dawn to shoot some desert-partridges in which the oasis abounds. Ere day broke I rose, and leaving the whole camp in slumber, strolled away to a rocky spot I had on the previous day noted as a likely place to find the birds. It was on the edge of the oasis, at some distance from the well where we had encamped. When I arrived there the sun had not risen, and the birds were still roosting. Therefore, with my rifle loaded with a bullet (for I had no small shot), I sat down to wait.

For perhaps half-an-hour I had remained when my quick ear detected the sounds of horses' hoofs. Believing the newcomer to be a French vedette I drew back behind a large boulder, with the barrel of my rifle placed upon the top of the rock in readiness to pick him off as he passed. On came the horseman, until suddenly he emerged from among the mimosas and euphorbias. An ejaculation of dismay involuntarily left my lips. There was not one horse, but two. The riders were fugitives. They were our prisoner-of-war, Lieutenant de Freyville, and Gabrielle Bonnemain, the woman I loved.

Mounted upon horses they had secured, they spurred forward together at headlong speed. Their way on to the desert lay down a narrow stony ravine, to traverse which they would be compelled to pass close by the spot where I was lying in ambush. On they came swiftly, without a word. Inwardly I gloated over my revenge.

This man was stealing from me the woman I loved dearer than life. And she—she had declared that she loved me! Yet her words were foul lies. She should die!

I fingered the trigger, and held my gun to my shoulder in readiness as the pair pressed forward, unconscious of their approaching doom. If ever the spirit of murder entered my soul, it was at that moment.

When within a leopard's leap of the muzzle of my rifle she turned back towards her companion, uttered some gay words to him, threw back her head and laughed lightly, displaying her white teeth.

I raised my rifle and took deliberate aim at her panting breast. My hands trembled. Next second a flood of bitter recollections surged through my brain. I remembered those solemn words she had uttered: "We are of different races; different creeds. What is right in thine eyes is sin in mine; what is worship to thee is, to me, idolatry. It is the very fact that we love one another that should cause us to part and forget."

Yes, my enchantress had spoken the truth.

My hands were nerveless. I dropped my gun, the weapon with which I had so nearly taken her young life, and through a mist of gathering tears watched her ride rapidly away beside her newly-discovered lover, and disappear over the dune towards El Aghouat.

When she had gone, my head sank upon my breast and my teeth were set, for full well I knew that never again could I love any woman as truly as I had loved her. My pole-star, the light of my life, had for ever been extinguished.

Chapter Three.

The Secret of Sâ.

Through the very heart of the barren, naked Saharan country, that boundless sea of red-brown arid sands, which, like the ocean itself, is subject to fitful moods of calm and storm, there runs a deep rocky ravine which has ever been a mystery to geographers. It commences near the shore of Lake Tsâd, and extending for nearly eight hundred miles due north to Lake Melghir, is known as the Igharghar, and is the dried-up bed of a river, which, with its tributaries, once rendered this bare wilderness one of the most fertile spots on earth, but which, for upwards of two thousand years, has ceased to flow. Strangely enough, the country traversed by this great stony ravine is to-day the most arid and inhospitable in the world. The river, which, according to the legendary stories told in the market-places of the desert towns, must have been as mighty as the Nile, dried-up suddenly from some cause which has always puzzled geographers. A portion of its course, about two hundred miles, half filled with sand, has for ages been used as the caravan route between the city of Agades, the capital of the Aïr country, and Temasinin, at the foot of the Tinghert Plateau; but the remainder is of such a rocky character as to be impassable, and has on many occasions served us as ambush when fighting the Ouled Slimân marauders, our hereditary foes.

"MORE DESPERATE EACH MOMENT THE CONFLICT GREW."
P. 75.

On one of these expeditions we were encamped in the shadow of some great rocks, which had once been covered by the giant flood. Around us on every hand was the sandy, waterless waste, known by the ominous name of *Ur-immandess*, "He (Allah) heareth not," that is, is deaf to the cry of the way-laid traveller. It is a dismal tract, one of the most hot and arid in the whole of Northern Africa. The poison-wind blows almost continually, and the general appearance of the sand dunes is altered almost hour by hour. We were six days' march off an interesting little walled town I had once visited, called Azaka 'n Ahkar, where stands the curious tomb of a chieftain who fell during the Arab invasion over a thousand years ago, and to the west, within sight, was the low dark hill known to us as Mount Hikena, a spot feared universally throughout the desert as the abode of the jinns.

Already had we engaged the fierce host of the Ouled Slimân in deadly conflict at the well of Agnar, but finding our opponents armed with rifles procured from European traders, we had drawn off in an endeavour to entice them into the Wady Igharghar, where our superior knowledge of the ground would give us distinct advantage. Our losses three days before had been very serious, and our Sheikh Tamahu had despatched messengers in all haste to the oasis of Noum-en-Nas, six marches distant, to urge forward reinforcements. That night, when the moon had risen, I accompanied Hamoud, one of my companions, as scout, to travel northward along the dried-up watercourse, to make a *reconnaissance*, and to ascertain if the enemy were in the vicinity. To ride up that valley, choked by its myriad boulders, was impossible, therefore we were compelled to journey on foot.

Had we ascended to the desert we should have imperilled our camp, for our enemies in search of us would undoubtedly detect our presence. We had pitched our tents at a secluded inaccessible spot, where the dried-up river had taken a sudden bend, in the heart of a country scarcely ever traversed. Through the long brilliant night with my companion I pressed forward, sometimes clambering over rough rocks, split by the heat of noon and chills of night, and at others sinking knee-deep in soft sand-drifts. When dawn spread we now and then clambered up the steep sides of the valley and cautiously took observations. In that region, the surface of the desert being perfectly flat, any object can be seen at great distances, therefore we at all times were careful not to stand upright, but remained crouched upon our faces. So dry also is the atmosphere that any sudden movement, such as the flapping of a burnouse or the swish of a horse's tail, will cause sparks to be emitted.

Beneath the milk-white sky of noon, when the fiery sun shone like a disc of burnished copper, we threw ourselves down beneath the shadow of a huge boulder to eat and rest. Hamoud, older than myself, was a typical nomad, bearded, bronzed, and a veritable giant in stature. His physical strength and power of endurance was greater than that of any other of our tribesmen, and he was always amiable and light-hearted. While he lit his keef-pipe and chatted, I gazed about me, noticing how, by the action of the eddying waters of this dried-up river, the very name of which is lost to us, the hard, grey rock above had been worn smooth and hollow. The mystery of the Igharghar had always attracted me since my earliest boyhood. Why this mighty stream, in some places nearly six miles wide, should have suddenly ceased to flow, fertilise, and give life to the great tract it traversed was a problem which the wise men of all ages had failed to solve. True, the One Merciful heard not in that wild, unfrequented region. It was the country accursed and forgotten of Allah.

When, in the cooler hours, we resumed our journey, ever-watchful for the presence of the Ouled Slimân, on every side we noticed unmistakable traces of the enormous width and depth of the giant waterway. About noon on the second day I had ascended to the desert to scan the horizon, when I discovered some ruined masonry, half-buried beneath its winding-sheet of sand. On the keystone of an arch I found an inscription in Roman characters, and here and there stood broken columns and portions of grey time-worn walls.

It was the site of an effaced and forgotten city; a centre of culture and civilisation which had owed its very existence to this great river, and had declined and fallen when the stream had so mysteriously ceased to flow. The once fertile land had withered, and become a dreary, sunburnt, uninhabitable wilderness.

Ask any marabout from Morocco to far-off Tripoli, and he will declare that for some reason unknown, Allah, before the days of his Prophet, set the mark of his displeasure upon the country known to us as the Ahaggar. It is not, therefore, surprising that the Ouled Slimân, our enemies, should be known throughout the desert as the Children of Eblis.

As, spear in hand, I walked at Hamoud's side along that vanished fluvial basin, I discussed the probable causes of the sudden failure of that mighty flow. He suggested that its source might by some means have become exhausted; but geographers having ages ago disposed of that point, I explained to him how every theory possible had already been put forward and dismissed. The mysterious forgotten river was still a geographical problem as great as the existence of open water at the poles.

Through two more days we journeyed forward, ever-watchful, yet discerning no sign of our enemies; but at length, coming to a steep bare cliff, once undoubtedly a roaring cataract, we found its granite bed had been worn into ridges two thousand years ago by the action of the torrent. At this point the plateau over which we had journeyed descended sheer and steep on to the plain, of which we commanded an extensive view for many miles. An hour before sundown the sky had suddenly darkened, indicative of an approaching sandstorm, therefore we resolved to remain there the night and retrace our steps next day. Our fears were realised. Shortly before midnight, as we sat together smoking, the unclouded starry sky assumed an extraordinary clearness. The atmosphere was perfectly still, when suddenly in the east a black cloud began to rise with frightful rapidity, and soon covered half the heavens. Presently a strong gust of wind enveloped us with sand, and threw little pebbles as large as peas into our faces. Soon, while we crouched beneath a rock, we were surrounded by a dense cloud of sand, and stood still in impenetrable gloom. The storm was of unusual severity. Our eyes were filled with grit every time we ventured to open them. We did not dare to lie down for fear of being buried. The tempest at last passed, the night quickly grew clear again, and, extricating ourselves from the sand that had drifted high about us, we lay down exhausted to sleep.

Before dawn I rose, and, without disturbing the heavy slumber of my companion, strode forth along the brink of the dried-up cataract to examine more closely the hitherto unexplored spot. The sun-whitened boulders were all worn smooth where the gigantic rush of the waters had whirled past them ere they dashed below into that once fertile plain. And as I went along I presently discovered a place where I could descend the face of the cliff. Without difficulty I at last reached its base, and stepping forward, placed my foot upon soft drifted sand that gave way beneath my tread.

With startling suddenness a strange sound fell upon my ears, deafening me. I felt myself falling, and in clutching frantically at the objects around, struck my head a violent blow. Then all consciousness became blotted out.

How long I remained insensible I do not know. I have an idea that many hours must have elapsed, for when painfully I struggled back to a knowledge of things about me, I found myself enveloped in a darkness blacker than night, my ears being filled by a continuous unceasing roar like thunder. I was chilled to the bone, and on stretching forth my hand, found myself lying upon a mass of soft slime, that splashing over my face had half-suffocated me. With both hands outstretched, I tried to discover into what noisome place I had so suddenly been precipitated. Intently I listened. The roaring was that of some mighty unseen torrent.

Creeping cautiously forward upon my hands and knees, fearing lest I should stumble into any further chasm, I soon came to water flowing swiftly past. Then the truth dawned upon me that I was beside the bank of some unknown subterranean river. Of the extent of that dark cavernous place I could obtain no idea. Thrice I shouted with all my strength, but in that deafening roar my voice was echoless.

With a supplication to Allah to envelop me with the cloak of his protection, I cautiously pursued my way over the stones and slime in the direction the unseen stream was rushing. The incline was steep, and as the air seemed cool and fresh, I felt assured there must be some outlet to the blessed light of day. Yet onward I crept slowly, chilled by the icy mud, until my limbs trembled, and I was compelled to pause and rub them to prevent them becoming benumbed.

Truly mine was an unenvious position. Throughout my life it has been my endeavour to tread those crooked and laborious paths whereby knowledge of hidden mysteries may be gained, therefore I worked on like a mole in the dark, and by diligent industry gained ground considerably. During several hours I pushed my way forward, until at length my hands came into contact with a wall of rock which barred all further passage, although the water lapping it swirled past on its downward course. Eagerly I felt about the rock, searching for some mode of egress, but could find none. The wall of the enormous cavern extended sheer and unbroken for five hundred paces, then turned back in the direction I had already traversed. Thus was a terrible truth forced upon me. I was entombed!

My injured head pained me frightfully, and I must have become weakened by loss of blood. The terrors of that foul, fearsome place, where the deafening roar was unceasing, and the blackness could be felt, overwhelmed me. I groped back to the edge of the roaring torrent exhausted, and sinking, slept.

When I awoke I was amazed to find the cavern illumined by a faint greenish light, just sufficient to enable me to see that the rushing, foaming waters were of great width and volume, and that the cavern whence they came was low, but of vast extent. Then, turning towards the light, I found that it shone up through the water beyond the wall of rock which formed that side of the cave. At first the strange light puzzled me, but I soon ascertained that the subterranean river emptied itself into the open air at that spot, and that the sun shining upon the water as it rushed out of its underground course, reflected the welcome light up to where I stood. The discovery held me breathless. I saw that in such enormous volume did those icy waters sweep down, that the opening in the rock whence they were let free was completely filled. There was, after all, no exit.

At the edge of the boiling torrent I stood calmly contemplating the advisability of plunging in and allowing myself to be swept out into the air. The only thing which deterred me from so doing was the fear that outside the cataract fell down from some dizzy height into a foaming flood below, in which case I must be either battered to death upon the rocks or drowned beneath the descending tons of water. The thought of this terrible fate thrilled me with horror.

Of a sudden I heard above the roar a man's voice; and startled, turned round, and saw a long boat, shaped something like a canoe, containing two dark figures, being propelled swiftly towards me.

Agape in wonder I stood watching them.

Ere I could realise the truth, they had run their craft up high and dry where I stood, and were beside me, questioning me in some strange, unknown tongue. In that faint green light they looked weird, impish figures. Small of stature, their skins were a lightish yellow; they wore curious necklets and armlets of chased bones, and their loincloths were scaly, like the skin of some fish or serpent. In their hands they both carried long barbed spears. They had been fishing, for their boat was nearly full.

To their rapid questions I could only shake my head, when in an instant the roar of the waters increased, until speech became impossible. Terrified they both, next second, leaped into their boat and dragged me in after them. Their promptitude saved my life, for ere an instant had elapsed our boat became lifted by an enormous inrush, which flooded the whole cavern to a depth of many feet. Our boat rose so near the roof that we were compelled to crouch down to prevent our heads being jammed, and soon I found myself being rowed rapidly along in triumph into the impenetrable darkness. I had escaped death by a hair's breadth, but what grim adventure was yet in store for me I dreaded to anticipate.

My impish captors bent hard at their paddles, exchanging muttered words, until soon the roaring of the torrent sounded indistinct, and we found ourselves out upon a great subterranean lake of limitless extent. The eyes of my companions, accustomed to that appalling darkness, could discern objects where I could distinguish nothing. As we went forward the current became weaker, and now and then I felt a splashing as a large fish was lifted from the water impaled upon a spear. Yet ever forward we kept on and on, for fully two hours, until suddenly I saw a faint glimmer of grey light upon the wide expanse of black water, and when we neared it I discerned that there was a huge crack in the roof of rock and it was open to the sky, but so great was the distance to the world above, that only a faint glimmer penetrated there.

By its light I distinguished how clear and deep were the waters, and noticed that the fish my companions had caught were of a uniform grey colour, without eyes. In the impenetrable darkness of those subterranean depths the organs of vision, I afterwards ascertained, never developed. The eyes of the two men with me were also strange-looking, set closely together, dark and bead-like.

But we paused not, holding straight upon our way, plunging again into the cavernous blackness, until presently there showed before us a golden shaft of sunlight striking full into the waters, and in a few moments we emerged into an open space green and fertile, surrounded on every side by high rocks, honeycombed with small caves, while the great unknown river itself disappeared beyond into a wide dark tunnel.

Scarcely had we disembarked than the place literally swarmed with the uncanny-looking denizens of this underground realm, who, issuing from their cave-dwellings, eyed me curiously with greatest caution. I had not removed my *litham*, and they undoubtedly were suspicious of a stranger who veiled his face.

My captors, with much wild gesticulation, explained the circumstances in which they had discovered me, and presently, when I had been thoroughly inspected by all, and my appearance commented upon, my veil was surreptitiously snatched from my pallid face, and I was hurried into one of the small cell-like caverns, and there secured to the rock by a rudely constructed chain. Soon food was brought me, and the inhabitants of the curious unknown country formed a ring near the river bank, and commenced to execute a kind of wild dance, accompanied by fiendish yells, working themselves into a frenzy, like the dancers of the Ouled Naïls. For a long time I watched their weird pantomimic gyrations, when at length my eyes were startled at beholding, in the centre of the circle, a tall man of much paler complexion than my own, dressed in a few dilapidated rags. Once or twice only I caught a glimpse of him, and then I recognised that his face was that of an European, and his dress the tattered remains of a French military uniform. His beard and moustache seemed ashen grey, and upon his haggard countenance, as he stood motionless and statuesque amid the dancers, was a weary look of blank despair. He also was a captive.

The strange-looking, yellow-skinned people of this riparian region at length ceased dancing, and with one accord knelt around him in adoration, worshipping him as though he were an idol. The scene, as they gabbled words in an unknown tongue, was weird and impressive. My fellow-captive did not apparently notice me, therefore, fearing to rouse the ire of this hitherto undiscovered people by shouting, I possessed myself in patience. The curious form of pagan worship at last ended; the unfortunate European was released and allowed to seek his abode, a small hole in the rock close to mine, and the impish-looking men dispersed, leaving me to my own dismal thoughts. Ere long the shadows lengthened as the sun sank behind the high rocks, and dusk crept on. About the open space which served as street, men and women of the curious tribe squatted, smoked, and chattered, while others, entering their boats armed with fishing-spears, paddled off down the subterranean stream in the direction I had come. Night fell, and at last the cave-dwellers slept.

Slumber, however, came not to my wearied eyes, and for many hours I sat thinking over my strange position, my thoughts being suddenly disturbed by a noise as of some one moaning near me. It was the mysterious European.

With slow steps and bent head he passed by, when, in a low clear voice, I accosted him in French.

Startled, he halted, peering towards me; and when I had uttered a few reassuring words, telling him that I was his fellow-captive, he came towards me, looking half-suspiciously into my face, and enquired my name.

I told him who I was, then made a similar enquiry.

"My name is Flatters," he answered in Arabic. "Thou mayest, perhaps, have heard of me in thy wanderings through the Desert?"

"Flatters!" I cried. "Art thou Colonel Flatters, the lost explorer whom the French have sought these three whole years?"

"The same," he answered, sighing deeply, his arms crossed over his breast. "For three years I have been held captive in this noisome Land of Sâ."

His tall dark figure stood out against the starlight, his head bowed in dejection. By this brave explorer's exploits the whole world had more than once been thrilled. By his intrepidity and ability to withstand the sudden extremes of heat and cold in our Great Desert, the French War Department had been enabled to complete their map of the Saharan plains. It was he who explored all the hitherto unknown region around El Biodh; who discovered and published explanations of the wonderful ruins of Tikbaben; who found the Afeli source; who climbed the mountain of Iraouen, and penetrated the country of the Ennitra, into which even we of the Azjar feared to venture. Twice he traversed the stony Tinghert tableland; but on the third occasion, while in the far south near Lake Tsâd, he suddenly disappeared, and although the French authorities had offered a reward of ten thousand francs to any one who could solve the mystery of his death or capture, and had sent two formidable expeditions across the desert, with a view of obtaining some tidings of him, all efforts had been futile.

Yet he had been here, a prisoner in the hands of these uncanny dwellers beneath the earth's surface!

"Hast thou made no attempt to escape?" I enquired, as he seated himself wearily upon a ledge of rock near me.

"Yes," he answered despondently; "but my diaries and geological collections have been lost. All egress from this place is closed. Yon rocks are too sheer and high to be scaled, and the black flood hath risen so that there is neither entrance nor exit."

Briefly, I told him the manner in which I found myself in that dark cavern with its noisy torrent, and when I had finished he explained the manner in which he had disappeared.

"I set forth from Algiers with five European companions, and after travelling for nine months along unfrequented paths in the inhospitable Ahaggar, found myself at Mount El Aghil alone, all my fellow-travellers having died. Unable to return by the route I had come on account of the fierce hostility of the Kel-Rhela, whose vengeance I had narrowly escaped, I was compelled to push on still southward through the Aïr country, reaching at last, close to the dried-up course of the Igharghar, a large and curious oasis, the earth of which was perfectly black and quite soft, contrasting strangely with the dull red sand of the surrounding desert. The vegetation was luxuriant, water-melons grew in rich profusion, and in exploring it I discovered, to my astonishment, a small but beautiful lake. About the oasis were large rocks, and in one of these I found an opening with curious signs rudely curved at the entrance. They appeared to be the hieroglyphics of some ancient race, and their strange character aroused my curiosity. Unlike any hitherto discovered, they were of huge design, representing men, monstrosities, and animals of unknown species, yet only superficially outlined, apparently with the most inadequate tools. Not only were they at the entrance, but on lighting a torch I found the interior of the cavern completely covered by these grotesque drawings; and it was while engaged in these interesting investigations that I suddenly stumbled into a narrow chasm that had evidently been hidden by dried branches to form a pitfall for the unwary. When I recovered consciousness I, like thyself, found myself captive in the hands of these fierce primitive barbarians of the nether world."

"But who are they?" I enquired. "I have never heard mention of them before."

"Nor I," he answered. "To our world they are as absolutely unknown as this mighty subterranean flood. During my captivity I have managed to learn some words of their tongue. Their gloomy, mysterious region is known to them as Sâ."

"But the river itself amazes me," I observed.

"True. Our accidental discoveries have proved an important geographical fact hitherto undreamed-of, namely, that the reason the mighty Igharghar no longer flows to irrigate the desert is because it has found a subterranean channel, and for ages has been still roaring on beneath its ancient bed towards the sea."

"Whence, in your opinion, cometh this mysterious river?" I enquired.

"From Lake Tsâd, undoubtedly. The fish in its waters, although grey and sightless, because of the perpetual darkness in which they live, are of the same species as those I found in the lake. The strangest part of my adventure is that these people, never having before seen a white man, believe me to be some supernatural visitant, and worship me as Sâ, their principal god."

Then, while he listened attentively, I told him of the cavern where the river apparently rushed out into the open air, and suggested that, as a desperate and last resource, we might endeavour to escape by plunging into the chilly stream and allowing ourselves to be carried forth into the unknown. On due consideration, however, we agreed that this project was not feasible, on account of the swollen state of the dark flood, and as an alternative resolved to steal one of the canoes and explore the upper reaches of the mysterious underground stream. This decision we followed by immediate action. The explorer, obtaining a roughly fashioned hammer of stone from his own little cave, quickly severed my fetters, and together we crept out across the small deserted grass-plain to where the boats were moored. In one of them we found paddles, torches and spears, and, stepping in, pushed off and shot silently out into the darkness. Ere we had done so, however, we heard a loud ringing shout close to the bank. Our flight had been discovered.

We each seized a paddle and pulled away with all our might against the stream. Quickly we entered the cavern opposite that through which I had been conveyed. The blackness was complete, but we strained every muscle in our efforts to propel forward our frail craft. Soon behind us we heard the wild, fierce yells of our pursuers, and knowing that their eyes, accustomed to that appalling gloom, could discern objects where we of the outer world could detect nothing, we feared lest we might be overtaken. Their angry voices echoed weirdly along the rocky roof, and we could hear the violent splashing of their paddles as they sped along in our wake.

In this mad dash into the unknown realm of perpetual night we shot forward with utter disregard of what dangers lay before. We knew not, from one moment to another, whether we were heading up the great broad river, or whether rowing straight towards the rocky sides of the cavern. So light and flimsy was our craft that the least collision with a piece of jutting rock would have sent us down to depths unfathomable. At that moment we were enveloped by an hundred perils.

To our surprise and profound satisfaction, we at length realised that the voices of our irate pursuers were growing fainter. They had evidently mistaken the direction we had taken, therefore we slowed up, and presently rested, spent and panting.

I could hear the French officer's hard breathing, but the darkness was so intense that we could not see each other.

"We have unconsciously entered a tributary of the main stream," he observed, gasping for breath. "Listen, the sounds are receding. At least for the present we are safe. Let us rest."

Nothing loth, I bent slowly across my paddle, now and then pulling a few strokes to prevent us drifting, and discussing our position in a low voice so that no echo should betray our presence. Thus we remained fully half-an-hour, until both of us had refreshed ourselves, then together we paddled on swiftly, yet full of caution. No glimmer of light penetrated that dispiriting gloom, and we feared to ignite one of our torches. Toiling forward, the perspiration rolling off us in great beads, we still continued pulling against the strong current for several hours, until suddenly we saw before us two large shafts of brilliant light striking down from above into the water. Slowly we approached lest any of the denizens of Sâ should be lurking there; but ere long, as we came nearer, our eyes were dazzled by a sight so amazing that expressions of wonder involuntarily escaped our parched lips.

In the light before us we saw clearly outlined a colossal face with hideous grin, carved from the black rock. It was truly gigantic, marvellously fashioned, with huge ears and an expression absolutely demoniacal, the two shafts of bright light issuing forth from the eyes giving it an expression of intense ferocity. We rested on our paddles beneath it, and looked up aghast.

"This," cried Colonel Flatters, "must be the god Sâ, of whom I have heard so much during my sojourn with these people. He is their principal deity, and supposed to be the inexorable guardian of this remarkable kingdom."

"See!" I exclaimed, regarding the extraordinary stone countenance in amazement. "The light from those eyes is sunlight! They are merely holes upon which the sun is shining full!"

And such it proved to be. Through the round apertures far up above, light and air were admitted from the desert.

When at last our vision became accustomed to the welcome rays of light we made another bewildering discovery. The rock descended sheer into the black flood, but in little niches which had been rudely fashioned lay small heaps of gold ornaments and glittering gems, the sacrifices of this stone god's votaries. Together we pulled our canoe close to the rock, taking care that the rapid swirl of the current did not hurl our craft against the jagged stones, and with my hand I clutched a heap of fine ornaments set with emeralds, pearls, and diamonds. In the sunlight we both examined them, finding they were evidently of very ancient manufacture, possibly the spoils of war against some long-forgotten but cultured nation. In workmanship they were similar to the ornaments found in the tombs of ancient Egypt; they had evidently never been manufactured by the barbarous people into whose possession they had passed.

Before us was blackness impenetrable, and upon our ears there broke a distant roar, as of a cataract. The sound appalled us. If a cataract actually lay before, then escape was absolutely hopeless.

But the fact that far above gleamed the sun gave us renewed courage, and after some discussion we became convinced that, this colossal face being regarded as the guardian of the unexplored country, an exit existed there. After some difficulty we ignited one of our torches, and with it stuck in the bows of the canoe, rode backwards and forwards, minutely examining the base of the rock. Once we passed so near that my companion was able to secure a handful of gems for himself, and both of us secreted these stolen votive offerings about our garments. The two parallel shafts of light from the eyes of the graven monstrosity, striking deep into the river, revealed curious fish and water-snakes disporting themselves around the boat, while great black bats which had come in through the two openings, startled by our presence, circled about us ominously with wide-spread flapping wings.

The water glittering beneath the torch's uncertain rays, flowed past so swiftly, that we were compelled to continue pulling in order to remain abreast of the idol. Long and earnestly we both searched to find some means by which we could reach the two holes that formed the idol's eyes; yet they seemed so small that it was questionable whether, even if we successfully clambered up the sculptured face, we could squeeze our bodies through. A dozen times we allowed the canoe to drift past, while I endeavoured to discover some means by which to reach those glaring eyes. But the bright sunlight dazzled us, and beyond the tiny niches filled with jewels there was no other inequality to serve as foothold to gain the narrow ledge which formed the lips. Again, if I made a false step I should be instantly swept away by the swirling current, and lost for ever in the dark whirling flood.

At length however my companion, muscular and agile, succeeded in springing clear of the canoe and gripping one of the small niches, tossing the jewels into the water by his frantic efforts. For an instant he struggled, his legs dangling in mid-air; then presently his toes found foothold, and he commenced slowly to clamber up the chin of the gigantic visage towards a kind of long ledge. I watched his progress breathlessly, not daring to utter a word, but keeping the canoe in readiness to row after him if he fell. With difficulty he ascended, clinging on to the face of the rock until he reached the great grinning mouth and stood up facing me.

"What do you find?" I shouted, my voice echoing weirdly. I had noticed that as he glanced along the spot where he stood his face became transfixed by horror.

"Follow me!" he replied hoarsely. "Have a care, a single false step means death."

At that instant the boat was passing the spot where he had gripped the rock's face, and without hesitation I followed his example and sprang, clutching the narrow slippery ledge with both hands. My feet found a resting-place, yet next second a thought which crossed my mind held me appalled. I had omitted to moor the boat.

Over my shoulder I throw a hasty glance. It had already drifted out of sight.

I heard my white companion shouting, but taking no heed toiled on up the great face until a strong helping hand gripped mine, and I found myself standing beside him upon the narrow ledge forming the lips of the hideous countenance.

Next instant, glancing round, my eyes encountered a sight which hold me petrified.

A long dark aperture, about the height of myself, formed the mouth, and set therein were broad sharp teeth of rusted sword-blades, which overlapping, prevented entrance to the cavernous throat. Twenty blades were set in the jaw above and twenty below, forming an impassable barrier of razor-edged spikes. Our only means of escape being cut off by the drifting of the canoe, one fact alone remained to give us courage. From where we stood we recognised the utter impossibility of passing through, the eyes of the colossus, yet, as together we looked at the formidable teeth, we saw a human skeleton lying beneath them. The skull was beyond the row of blades, the legs towards us, proving that some means existed by which those jaws could be opened. The unfortunate man had, apparently, been impaled by the descending blades while in the act of escaping.

After brief consultation we began an active search to discover the means by which the mouth could be opened. What lay beyond in that dark cavernous throat we knew not, though we strained our eyes into the blackness, and shook the sharp steel spikes in a vain endeavour to loosen them. For a full hour we searched, discovering nothing to lead us to any solution of the problem. That freedom lay beyond we felt convinced, by reason of the light and air from above; but whatever were the means employed to raise the deadly jaw they were a secret. Time after time we examined every nook and crevice minutely, until at last, when just about to give up our search as futile, I suddenly espied, projecting from the river's surface, a short bar of iron, with the appearance of a lever.

To reach it was imperative, therefore at imminent risk I let myself carefully over the edge of the rock, slowly lowering my body until I could grip it. Beneath my weight it slowly gave way, and next instant there was a loud gurgling as of water drawn in by a vacuum, followed immediately by a harsh metallic grating sound.

"At last!" I heard the Colonel cry in French. "It rises! Be careful how you ascend."

Slowly, and with infinite care, I crept upward, but as I did so I heard my companion's echoing footsteps receding into the gloomy throat of Sâ, yet just as I had gained the ledge forming the lips I heard a piercing shriek, followed by a loud splash.

I shouted, but there was no answer. My companion had stumbled into some chasm, and I was alone. The light of the hideous eyes had died out, and the spot was in almost total darkness. A dozen times I called his name, but there was no reassuring reply. Then, cautiously creeping forward upon my hands and knees, fearing the worst, I soon came to the edge of an abyss. Some stones I gathered and flung in. By the sound of the splash I knew the water must be of enormous depth. There, in that dark uncanny spot, had Colonel Flatters, the great explorer, whose intrepidity has been for years admired by the world, met his death.

A long time I spent alternately shouting and listening. He might, I reflected, have been saved by falling stunned upon some rocky ledge. But I remembered hearing the splash. No, he had undoubtedly been precipitated into the water: the inky flood had closed over him.

After diligent search I found a spot where the abyss ended, and again crept forward, still in darkness most intense. Yet the air seemed fresh, and I felt convinced that some outlet must lay beyond. How long, however, I toiled on in that narrow tunnel I know not, save that its dampness chilled me; and when at last it widened in ascending, I found myself a few minutes afterwards amid brushwood and brambles in the outer world.

That night I wandered across the large fertile tract, but could not at first recognise it. When dawn spread, however, I saw around me a ridge of dunes that were familiar landmarks, and recognised, to my amazement, that I was at the oasis of Am Ohannan, on the direct caravan route that runs across the barren Afelèle to Touat.

I had travelled nearly seventy miles in a subterranean region unknown to man, but in so doing had solved the problem that had so long puzzled geographers, the reason why the Igharghar no longer flowed. Besides, I had ascertained the fate of the hapless explorer, whose loss is lamented by both Arabs and Roumis to this day. Within one moon of my escape I was enabled to rejoin my people, and when news of my adventure reached the Bureau Arabe, in Algiers, I was summoned thither to give a detailed account of it before a small assembly of geographers and military officers.

This I did, a report of it appearing in English in *The Geographical Journal* a month later. Of late, several attempts have been made by French expeditions to reach that uncanny realm of eternal darkness, but without success. Its entrance beneath the dry cataract of the Igharghar is now merely an overflowing well, around which a little herbage has grown, while its exit on the Am Ohannan I have unfortunately failed to re-discover. But since this strange adventure I have been known among my fellow tribesmen throughout the desert as "El Waci," or The

Teacher, because I have been enabled to prove to the French the existence of an undreamed-of region, and to elucidate the Secret of Sâ.

Chapter Four.

The Three Dwarfs of Lebo.

When my beard, now long, scraggy, and grey, was yet soft as silk upon my youthful chin, I was sent as spy into Agadez, the mysterious City of the Black Sultan. At that time it was the richest, most zealously guarded, and most strongly fortified town in the whole Sahara, and surrounded, as it constantly was, by marauding tribes and enemies of all sorts, a vigilant watch was kept day and night, and woe betide any stranger found within its colossal walls, for the most fiendish of tortures that the mind of man could devise was certain to be practised upon him, and his body eventually given to the hungry dogs at the city gate.

In order, however, to ascertain its true strength and the number of its garrison, I, as one of the younger and more adventurous of our clansmen, was chosen by Tamahu, our Sheikh, to enter and bring back report to our encampment in the rocky fastness of the Tignoutin. Therefore I removed my big black veil, assumed the white haik and burnouse of the Beni-Mansour, a peaceful tribe further north, and contrived to be captured as slave by a party of raiding Ennitra who were encamped by the well of Tafidet, five miles from the capital of Ahir. As I had anticipated, I was soon taken to the City of the Black Sultan, and there sold in the slave-market, first becoming the property of a Jew merchant, then of Hanaza, the Grand Vizier of the Sultan. As personal slave of this high official I was lodged within the palace, or Fada, that veritable city within a city, containing as it did nearly three thousand inhabitants, over one thousand of whom were inmates of his Majesty's harem.

In the whole of Africa, no monarch, not even the Moorish Lord of the Land of the Maghrib, was housed so luxuriously as this half-negro conqueror of the Asben. When first I entered the Fada as slave, I was struck by the magnificence of the wonderful domain. As I crossed court after court, each more beautiful than the one before, and each devoted to a separate department of the royal household, the guards, the janissaries, the treasurer, the armourers, and the eunuchs, I was amazed at every turn by their magnificence and beauty. At last we came to the court of the Grand Vizier, a smaller but prettier place, with a cool, plashing fountain tiled in blue and white, and shaded by figs, myrtles, and trailing vines. Beyond, I could see an arched gateway in the black wall, before which stood two giant negro guards in bright blue, their drawn swords flashing in the sun. Of my conductor I enquired whither that gate led, and was told it was impassable to all save the Sultan himself, for it was the gate of the Courts of Love, the entrance to the royal harem.

Through the many months during which I served my capricious master, that closed, iron-studded door, zealously guarded night and day by its mute janissaries with their curved scimitars, was a constant source of mystery to me. Often I sat in the courtyard and dreamed of the thousand terrible dramas which that ponderous door hid from those outside that world of love, hatred, and all the fiercest passions of the human heart. The Sultan was fickle and capricious. The favourite of to-day was the discarded of to-morrow. The bright-eyed houri who, loaded with jewels, could twist her master round her finger one day, was the next the merest harem slave, compelled to wash the feet of the woman who had succeeded her in her royal master's favour. Truly the harem of the Sultan of the Ahir was a veritable hotbed of intrigue, where ofttimes the innocent victims of jealousy were cast alive to the wild beasts, or compelled to partake of the Cup of Death—coffee wherein chopped hair had been placed—a draught that was inevitably fatal.

One brilliant night, when the silver moonbeams whitened the court wherein I lived, I sat in the deep shadow of the oleanders, sad and lonely. Through six long dreary months had I been held slave by the Grand Vizier, yet it was Allah's will that I should have no opportunity to return to my people. So I possessed myself in patience. Through those months mine eyes and ears had been ever on the alert, and long ago I had completed my investigations. Suddenly my reflections were interrupted, for I saw standing before me a veritable vision of beauty, a pale-faced girl in the gorgeous costume of the harem, covered with glittering jewels, and wearing the tiny fez, pearl-embroidered zouave, and filmy *serroual* of the Sultan's favourites. Not more than eighteen, her unveiled countenance was white as any Englishwoman's; her startled eyes were bright as the moonbeams above, and as she stood mute and trembling before me, her bare, panting bosom, half-covered by her long, dark tresses, rose and fell quickly. I raised my eyes, and saw that the negro guards were sleeping. She had escaped from the Courts of Love.

"Quick!" she gasped, terrified. "Hide me, while there is yet time."

At her bidding I rose instantly, for her wondrous beauty held me as beneath some witch's spell. And at the same time I led the way to my tiny den, a mere hole in the gigantic wall that separated the royal harem from the outer courts of the palace.

"My name is Zohra," she explained, when she had entered; "and thine?"—she paused for an instant, looking me straight in the face. "Of a verity," she added at length, "thine is Ahamadou, the spy of the dreaded Azjar, the Veiled Men."

I started, for I had believed my secret safe.

"What knowest thou of me?" I gasped eagerly.

"That thou hast risked all in order to report to thy people upon the Black Sultan's strength," she answered, sinking upon my narrow divan, throwing back her handsome head and gazing into my eyes. "But our interests are mutual. I have these ten months been held captive, and desire to escape. By bribing one of the slaves with the Sultan's ring I contrived to have poison placed in the kouss-kouss of the guards—"

"You have killed them!" I cried, peering forth, and noticing the ghastly look upon their faces as they slept at their posts.

"It was the only way," she answered, shrugging her shoulders. "To obtain me the Sultan's men murdered my kinsmen, and put our village to the sword. Mine is but a mild revenge."

"Of what tribe art thou?" I enquired eagerly, detecting in her soft sibillations an accent entirely unfamiliar.

"I am of the Kel-Oui, and was born at Lebo."

"At Lebo!" I cried eagerly. "Then thou knowest of the Three Dwarfs of Lebo?"

"Yea. And furthermore I have learnt their secret, a secret which shall be thine alone in return for safe conduct to my people."

"But my clansmen are in deadly feud with thine," I observed reflectively.

"Does that affect thy decision?" she enquired in a tone of reproach.

I reflected, and saw how utterly impossible it seemed that I myself could escape the vigilance of these ever-watchful guards of the many gates which lay between myself and freedom. I glanced at the frail girl lying upon my poor ragged divan, her girdle and throat blazing with jewels, and felt my heart sink within me.

"Thou thinkest that because I am a woman I have no courage," she observed, her keen eyes reading my secret thoughts. "But hist! listen!"

I held my breath, and as I did so the footsteps of men fell upon the flags of the courtyard. We peered forth through the chink in the wooden shutter, which at night closed my window, and saw two men carrying a bier, followed by two gigantic negro eunuchs. Upon the bier was a body covered by a cloth; and as it passed we both caught sight of gay-coloured silks and lace. Below the black pall a slim white hand, sparkling with diamonds, moved convulsively, and as the *cortège* passed, a low stifling cry reached us—the despairing cry of a woman.

"All!" gasped my companion, dismayed. "It is Zulaimena! Yesterday she ruled the harem, but this morning it was whispered into our lord's ear that she had tried to poison him, and he condemned her and myself to be given alive to the alligators," and she shuddered at thought of the fate which awaited her if detected.

Conversing only in whispers, we waited till the palace was hushed in sleep. Then, when she had attired herself in one of my old serving-dresses and bound her hair tightly, we crept cautiously out into the moonlit court. Over the horse-shoe arch of the harem-gate the single light burned yellow and faint, while on either side the guards crouched, their dead fingers still grasping their ponderous scimitars. All was still, therefore quietly and swiftly we passed into the Court of the Treasury, and thence into that of the Eunuchs. Here we were instantly challenged by two guards with drawn swords, clansmen of those who lay dead at the harem-gate.

"Whence goest thou?" they both enquired with one voice, suddenly awakened from gazing mutely at the stars, their blades flashing in the moonbeams.

"Our master, the Grand Vizier, has had an apoplexy, and is dying!" I cried, uttering the first excuse that rose to my lips. "Let not his life be upon thine heads, for we go forth to seek the court physician Ibrahim."

"Speed on the wings of haste!" they cried. "May the One Merciful have compassion upon him!"

Thus we passed onward, relating the same story at each gate, and being accorded the same free passage, until at last we came to an enormous steel-bound door which gave exit into the city; the gate which was closed and barred by its ponderous bolts at the *maghrib* hour, and opened not until dawn save for the dark faced Sultan himself.

Here I gave exactly the same account of our intentions to the captain of the guard. He chanced to be a friend of my master's, and was greatly concerned when I vividly described his critical condition.

"Let the slaves pass!" I heard him cry a moment later, and, with a loud creaking, the iron-studded door which had resisted centuries of siege and battle, slowly swung back upon its creaking hinges. At that instant, however, a prying guard raised his lantern and held it close to my companion's face.

"By the Prophet's beard, a woman!" he cried aloud, starting back, an instant later. "We are tricked!"

"Seize them!" commanded the captain, and in a moment three guards threw themselves upon us. Swift as thought I drew my keen *jambiyah*, my trusty knife which I had ever carried in my sash throughout my captivity, and plunged it into the heart of the first man who laid hands upon me, while a second later the man who gripped Zohra, received a cut full across his broad negro features which for ever spoilt his beauty. Then, with a wild shout to my companion to follow, I dashed forward and ran for my life.

Lithe and agile as a gazelle in the desert she sped on beside me along the dark crooked silent streets. In a few minutes the tragedy of the harem-gate would be discovered, and every effort would be then made to recapture the eloping favourite of the brutal Black Sultan. We knew well that if captured both of us would be given alive to the alligators, a punishment too terrible to contemplate. But together we sped on, our pace quickened by the fiendish yells of our pursuers, until doubling in a maze of narrow crooked streets, we succeeded at last, with Allah directing our footsteps, in evading the howling guards and gaining one of the four gates of the city, where the same story as we had told in the Fada resulted in the barrier being opened for us, and a moment later we found ourselves in the wild, barren plain, at that hour lying white beneath the brilliant moon. We paused not, however, to admire picturesque effects, but strode boldly forward, eager to put as great a distance as possible between ourselves and the stronghold of the Ahir, ere the dawn.

Fortunately my bright-eyed fellow-fugitive was well acquainted with the country around Agadez, therefore we were enabled to journey by untravelled paths; but the three days we spent in that burning inhospitable wilderness, ere we reached the well where we obtained our first handful of dates and slaked our thirst, were among the most terrible of any I have experienced during my many wanderings over the sandy Saharan waste.

On that evening when the mysterious horizon was ablaze with the fiery sunset, and I had turned my face to the Holy Ca'aba, I was dismayed to discover that, instead of travelling towards the country of her people, the Kel-Oui, we had struck out in an entirely different direction, but when I mentioned it she merely replied—

"I promised, in return for thine assistance, to lead thee unto the Three Dwarfs of Lebo, the secret of which none know save myself. Ere three suns have set thine eyes shall witness that which will amaze thee."

Next day we trudged still forward into a stony, almost impenetrable country, utterly unknown to me, and two days later, having ascended a rocky ridge, my conductress suddenly halted almost breathless, her tiny feet sadly cut by the sharp stones notwithstanding the wrappings I had placed about them, and pointing before her, cried—

"Behold! The Three Dwarfs!"

Eagerly I strained mine eyes in the direction indicated, and there discerned in the small oasis below, about an hour's march distant, three colossal pyramids of rock of similar shape to those beside the Nile.

"Yon fertile spot was Lebo until ten years ago, when the men of the Black Sultan came and destroyed it, and took its inhabitants as slaves," she explained. "See! From here thou canst distinguish the white walls of the ruins gleaming amongst the palms. We of the Kel-Oui had lived here since the days of the Prophet, until our enemies of the Ahir conquered us. But let us haste forward, and I will impart unto thee the secret I have promised."

Together we clambered down over the rocks and gained the sandy plain, at last reaching the ruined and desolate town where the cracked smoke-stained walls were half overgrown by tangled masses of greenery, welcome in that sunbaked wilderness, and presently came to the base of the first of the colossal monuments of a past and long-forgotten age. They were built of blocks of dark grey granite, sadly chipped and worn at the base, but higher up still well preserved, having regard to the generations that must have arisen and passed since the hands that built them crumbled to dust.

"By pure accident," explained the bright-faced girl when together we halted to gaze upward, "I discovered the secret of these wonders of Lebo. Thou hast, by thy lion's courage, saved my life, therefore unto thee is due the greatest reward that I can offer thee. Two years ago I fell captive in the hands of thy people, the Azjar, over in the Tinghert, and it was by thine own good favour I was released. That is why I recognised thee in the palace of Agadez. Now once again I owe my freedom unto thee; therefore, in order that the months thou hast spent in Agadez shall not be wholly wasted, I will reveal unto thee the secret which I have always withheld from mine own people."

Then, taking my hand, she quickly walked along the base of the giant structure until she came to the corner facing the direction of the sunrise;

then, counting her footsteps, she proceeded with care, stopping at last beneath the sloping wall, and examining the ground. At her feet was a small slab, hidden by the red sand of the desert, which she removed, drawing from beneath it a roll of untanned leopard-hide. This she unwrapped carefully, displaying to my gaze a worn and tattered parchment, once emblazoned in blue and gold, but now sadly faded and half illegible.

I examined it eagerly, and found it written in puzzling hieroglyphics, such as I had never before seen.

"Our marabout Ahman, who was well versed in the language of the ancients, deciphered this for me only a few hours before his death. It is the testimony of the great Lebo, king of all the lands from the southern shore of Lake Tsâd to the Congo, and founder of the Kel-Oui nation, now, alas! so sadly fallen from their high estate. The parchment states plainly that Lebo, having conquered and despoiled the Ethiopians in the last year of his reign, gathered together all the treasure and brought it hither to this spot, which bore his name, in that day a gigantic walled city larger by far than Agadez."

I glanced around upon the few miserable ruins of mud-built houses, and saw beyond them large mounds which, in themselves, indicated that the foundations of an important centre of a forgotten civilisation lay buried beneath where we stood.

"Lebo had one son," continued Zohra, "and he had revolted against his father; therefore the latter, feeling that his strength was failing, and having been told by the sorcerers that on his death his great kingdom would dwindle until his name became forgotten, resolved to build these three pyramids, that they should remain throughout all ages as monuments of his greatness."

"And the treasure?" I asked. "Is it stated what became of it?"

"Most precisely. It is recorded here," she answered, pointing to a half-defaced line in the mysterious screed. "The king feared lest his refractory son, who had endeavoured to usurp his power in the country many marches farther south, would obtain possession of the spoils of war, therefore he concealed them in one of yonder monuments."

"In there!" I cried eagerly. "Is the treasure actually still there?"

"It cannot have been removed. The secret lies in the apex of the third and lastly constructed monument," she explained.

"But the summit cannot be reached," I observed, glancing up at the high point. "It would require a ladder as long as that of Jacob's dream."

"There is a secret way," she answered quite calmly. "If thou art prepared for the risk, I am quite ready to accompany thee. Let us at once explore."

Together we approached the base of the third pyramid, and Zohra, after careful calculation and examination, led me to a spot where there was a hole in the stone just of sufficient size to admit a human foot. One might have passed it by unnoticed, for so cunningly was it devised that it looked like a natural defect in the block of granite.

"Behold!" she cried. "Climb, and I will follow."

The day was hot, and the sun had only just passed the noon, nevertheless I placed my foot in the burning stone, and scrambling forward found that she had made no mistake. At intervals there were similar footholds, winding, intricate, and in many instances filled with the nests of vultures, but always ascending. For fully half an hour we toiled upward to the apex, until we at length reached it, perspiring and panting, and minutely examined the single enormous block of stone that capped the summit. By its size I saw that no human hands could move it. If the treasure lay beneath, then it must remain for ever concealed.

"That parchment giveth no instructions how the spoils of war may be reached. We must discover that for ourselves," she observed, clambering on, still in her ragged male attire with which I had furnished her before leaving the stronghold of the Black Sultan.

I was clinging with one arm around the apex itself, and with the other grasping her soft white hand. She had looked down from the dizzy height and shuddered, therefore I feared lest she might be seized with a sudden giddiness. But quickly she released herself, and proceeded to scramble along on hands and knees, making a minute investigation of the wall.

Her sudden cry brought me quickly to her side, and my heart leapt wildly when I discerned before me, in the wall of the pyramid, immediately at the base of the gigantic block forming the apex, an aperture closed by a sheet of heavy iron, coloured exactly the same as the stone and quite indistinguishable from it. Some minutes we spent in its examination, beating upon it with our fists. But the secret how to open it was an enigma as great as that of the closed cavern in our book of the "Thousand Nights and a Night," until suddenly, by merest chance, we both placed our hands upon it, and it moved slightly beneath our touch. Next moment, with a cry, we both pushed our hardest, and slowly, ever so slowly, it slid along, grating in the groove, which was doubtless filled by the dust of centuries, disclosing a small, dark, low chamber roofed by the apex-stone.

Stepping inside, our gaze eagerly wandered around the mysterious place, and we at once saw that we had indeed discovered the treasure-house of Lebo the Great, for around us were piled a wondrous store of gold and gems, personal ornaments and great golden goblets and salvers. The aggregate value of the treasure was enormous.

"Of a verity," I cried, "this is amazing!"

"Yea," she answered, turning her fine eyes upon me. "I give this secret entirely and unreservedly unto thee, as reward for thine aid. At the going down of the sun I shall part from thee, and leave this home of my race for ever. In six hours' march, by the secret gorges, I can reach our encampment, therefore trouble no further after me. Close this treasure-house, return to thine own people, and let them profit by thy discovery."

"But thou, Zohra, boldest me in fascination," I cried passionately. "Thou hast entranced me. I love thee!"

"Love can never enter mine heart," she answered with a calm smile, but sighing nevertheless. "I am already the wife of thine enemy, Melaki, ruler of the Kel-Oui."

"Wife of Melaki!" I exclaimed amazed. "And thou hast done this?"

"Yes," she answered in a lower voice. "I have given thee thy promised reward, so that thou and thy people may become rich, and some day make brotherhood with us, and unite against the Black Sultan."

"If such is in my power it shall be done," I said, stooping and imprinting a passionate kiss upon her soft white hand. Then soon afterwards we closed the mouth of the chamber and descended, finding the task no easy one. At the base of the "Dwarf" we parted, and never since have mine eyes beheld her beautiful countenance.

Ere a moon had passed away, I had conducted a party of my clansmen unto the Three Dwarfs, and we had removed the treasure of the great founder of the Kel-Oui. Of such quantity was it that seven camels were required to convey it to Mourzouk, where it was sold to the Jews in the market, and fetched a sum which greatly swelled our finances.

True to my promise, when I assumed the chieftainship of the Azjar, I effected a friendly alliance with the Kel-Oui, and endeavoured to seek out Zohra.

But with poignant grief I learnt that soon after her return to her people she had been seized by a mysterious illness which proved fatal. Undoubtedly she was poisoned, for it was her evil-faced husband, Melaki, who told me how he had found in her possession a mysterious screed relating to the treasure of Lebo, and how, when questioned, she had admitted revealing its secret to the man who had rescued her from the harem of the Black Sultan.

Melaki never knew that the man with whom she fled from Agadez, and who loved her more devotedly than any other man had ever done, was myself.

Chapter Five.

The Coming of Allah.

One breathless evening, when the golden sun had deepened to crimson, and the shadows of the rocks were lengthening upon the white furnace of the sands, an alarm spread through our camp that strange horsemen were riding hard down the valley in our direction. Marauders that we were, fierce reprisals were of no infrequent occurrence, therefore the women and children were quickly hurried out of the way, the camels tethered, and each man gripped his spear, prepared to resist whatever onslaught might be made.

Along the Wady Ereren, six days' march south of the town of Ghat, where we were at that time encamped, we had taken the precaution to post three men in order to give us warning in case of any projected attack by the Kel-Alkoum, the powerful people with whom we were at feud on account of the murder of six of our clansmen up in the north of Fezzan. Our outposts, however, had sent us no word, therefore the only conclusion was that they had been surprised and killed ere they could reach us.

Hearing the news, I clambered up the bank of the ancient dried-up watercourse, in the bed of which we had pitched our tents, and, looking across the bend, we saw four dark specks approaching. The eye of the Touareg is as keen as that of the eagle, for, living as we do upon plunder, our intelligence becomes so sharpened that we somehow instinctively scent the approach of the stranger long before we see or hear him. In a few moments the men crowded about me for my opinion. Tamahu was dead, and this occurred in the first year of my chieftainship of the Azjar.

"Let all four be captured and brought to me," I said, my eyes still fixed upon the approaching figures. "If they resist, kill them."

In an instant twenty men, dark and forbidding in their black veils, sprang into their high-backed brass-mounted saddles, and with their gleaming spears held high, ready to strike, swept away down the valley to meet the new-comers.

Half an hour passed anxiously. The women in the rear chattered excitedly, and the children, held back by them, rent the air by their cries. From where I stood I was unable to witness the meeting of our men with the strangers, but suddenly the sound of firearms reached our ears. Then I felt assured that the mysterious horsemen must either be the advance-guard of some valuable caravan from Algeria, or of an army from the north. Yet again and again the guns spoke forth, and so rapidly that I feared for the safety of our men; but at last there was silence deep and complete, and when I descended to the camp I found a tumultuous excitement prevailing. The four men, escorted by those who had gone to arrest them, were still carrying their guns, and as they slipped from their saddles before me, smiles broadened their unveiled faces.

I looked at them puzzled. It seemed as though the firing had been but powder-play.

"Behold! O Ahamadou, our Sheikh! We are thy kinsmen, yet thou hast sent to attack us!" they exclaimed.

"Our kinsmen!" I cried, noticing that they wore the white burnouse of the north, with their *haicks* held around their heads by ropes of twisted camel's hair. They wore no veils, and a Touareg is unrecognisable, even to his relatives, if his black *litham* be removed.

"Yea," cried one, the elder of the four. "Lend us a veil, and we will show thee."

A strip of black cotton cloth was thrust into his hand by one of the crowd, and he assumed it, twisting it deftly as only a Touareg can. Then he turned and faced the onlookers, who with one accord laughed immoderately, hailing him as Taghma, son of Ifafan. Then the other three assumed the veil, and were, one by one, recognised and received back by their relatives.

At the conclusion of this strange ceremony, Taghma turned to me explaining how long ago before Ramadan they had wandered afar with their flocks to the oasis of Ezirer, and were there taken captives by the Kel-Alkoum.

"But," he added, "we have seen with our eyes the greatest wonder on earth. Allah himself hath come down from heaven!"

"What?" I cried, starting to my feet. "Thou liest!" The sensation caused by the man's calm announcement was intense.

"If my tongue uttereth falsehood, O Sheikh! then let it be cut out," he said. "I have seen Allah, the One. He guideth the Kel-Alkoum our enemies, and we are of a verity forsaken."

"Ah!" wailed the old marabout Ajrab. "Did I not warn ye that because of your inattention to your devotions and your neglect to say the five prayers, the One Merciful would leave you to perish and be eaten by the vultures like the lame camel in the wilderness?"

"Loose not thy tongue's strings," I commanded quickly. "Let us hearken unto Taghma, who hath seen the One from above."

"Of a verity, O Ahamadou!" answered the escaped captive, "we are lost, for Allah hath promised to render assistance unto the people he favoured in their expeditions. He declareth that we, of the Touaregs, are the parasites of the earth, and that we shall be exterminated, not one being left. Truly he can render our spears as broken reeds, and our blades as useless as rusted tin. Each day at the *maghrib* he standeth beneath a baldachin of purple and giveth the people an assurance of his favour, while all fall down and kiss the hem of his crimson garment so that they may be blessed. In Salemma, El Had, El Guerat, and the villages around Gatron, he hath healed the sick and performed wondrous miracles, while before our own eyes hath he caused a great tree to rise from the bare sand—a marvel which no earthly being could accomplish."

"The latter thou hast thyself seen?" I enquired, much interested in this most remarkable statement.

"We have, O Sheikh!" he answered. "The face of Allah is in the darkness as a shining light. Verily the promise in the *sura* is fulfilled. He hath come in person to lead the Faithful unto conquest."

Alone I sat in my tent that night, smoking and pondering deeply over the strange report. In the camp the excitement had already risen to fever-heat. The aged Ajrab was addressing the crowd of men and women, urging them to earnest supplication. Allah had come, and would vent his wrath upon those who had discarded His Book of Everlasting Will. From my divan I could hear the grey-bearded marabout's declaratory argument, and began to wonder whether the statement that Allah had descended upon earth had any foundation in fact. I confess to being sceptical. From the wailing of the women, and the low growls of the men, I knew plainly that the belief in the report must have a seriously disheartening effect upon our fighting men, who, if convinced that Allah assisted their enemies, would no doubt throw down their arms and flee.

I therefore saw that the statement of Taghma and his companions must be investigated, and after deep thought at length resolved to assume a disguise, and go myself to the camp of the Kel-Alkoum and see the miracles of which the men had spoken. To leave the Azjar without its Sheikh at such a time would, I knew, result disastrously; therefore, calling together the marabout and three of the most trusted headmen, I secretly explained to them my intention, and told them to account for my non-appearance during the next few days by spreading the report that I was seized by a slight fever and confined to my tent.

Then just before the waning of the moon, the dress that Taghma had worn was brought to me, and, assuming it, I mounted a fleet horse and set forth alone down the winding wady.

With the facts I had elicited from the four fugitives vivid within my mind, I journeyed forward, arriving ten days later in the little stone-built town of Zemnou, a cluster of white houses surrounding its small mosque capped by three thin whitewashed minarets. Wearing as I did the correct garb of a tribesman of the Kel-Alkoum, my presence was unnoticed, and I was therefore enabled to stroll about the market-places and make my observations while pretending to bargain for goods I had no intention of purchasing.

At sunset each day, when the voice of the *mueddin* sounded from the minaret, "Allah is great!" I crossed to the mosque, washed my feet in the marble basin and entered, in the expectation of seeing the Ruler of Earth, but was each day disappointed. At that hour the surrounding terraces were peopled with white forms, which stood out against the summits of the palm-trees and the green of the baobab. Their backs were turned to the purple splendours of the dying light, for their faces looked towards the already darkened east, lighted for us by that eternal light in which Mecca is to be found. At length, after a week had elapsed, a great and excited crowd gathered in the market, and, when I enquired its reason, I learned that Allah was coming.

For an hour we waited in the full glare of the noon-day sun, until suddenly a shout of joy arose, and all fell upon their knees in adoration. Then, lifting my eyes, I witnessed for the first time the One Merciful in the flesh. Truly Taghma had not lied. He was of middle-age, a trifle pale, but his dark eyes had a kindly, sympathetic look, and his countenance was open and bright, a face such as is never seen on earth. In his robe of blood-red he stood with his head uncovered, and while the people about him kissed his feet and the hem of his robe, he stretched forth both hands over them, pronouncing upon them his blessing and an assurance of his favour.

One fact, however, struck me as curious. Abreha, the Sheikh, stood aloof, with arms folded, watching the scene from beneath his shaggy brows. The glare in his keen eye told me that within his heart he concealed a fierce jealousy that his power had thus been eclipsed.

The people, frantic with joy at the words of the Giver of all Good Gifts, cried aloud their praises, repeating their *fâtihat*, and making open declaration of their belief. The scene was the strangest and most exciting that ever I had witnessed, for, carried away by their enthusiasm, many fell fainting, and were trampled upon by the crowd eagerly struggling to press Allah's garment to their lips, and obtain the remission of all past sins.

Suddenly the tall, erect, imposing figure in blood-red, truly kingly, raised both arms above his head, and, in a clear voice that echoed across the market above the clamours of the wild perspiring crowd, commanded silence. In an instant one could have heard a cricket chirp. Every mouth was open in breathless eagerness, for Allah was about to speak to them, his chosen, with his own lips.

"Give ear, O my well-beloved!" he cried, with an accent unfamiliar. "Among ye have I come because ye have repeated your *sûras* faithfully, and have believed in my Prophet. Of a verity will I bless you with abundant blessings, and the sun of my favour shall shine upon you so that your enemies may wither before the dazzling light shed by your faces. You, the Kel-Alkoum, my beloved, shall sweep from the face of the earth the wicked who have oppressed you, and their entrails will be burned by the all-consuming fire of my vengeance. The Touaregs, those who hide their faces in veils because of the hideousness of their iniquities, shalt thou put to the sword, and they shall be consigned to the place Al-Hâwiyat, where their food shall be offal, and melting pitch shall slake their thirst. I am thy leader, henceforward fear not, for thou hast a stronger hand than all nations of the earth, and at my will all who oppose thee shall be routed and die. The Kel-Alkoum, my chosen, shall rule the world."

He paused, and glanced round with an eye keen as a falcon's, while loud praises arose from every hoarse throat around.

"We will rout the Azjar from their mountain fastnesses!" they cried. "We are ready at any moment to do thy bidding, and sweep away the wicked. Thou wilt give strength to our arms that none can resist. Be praised, O King of earth and heaven! Be praised, O One!"

A smile of satisfaction played about the lips of the red-robed visitant from the unknown; but, without further word, he turned and stalked slowly to the mosque, the excited crowd closing in behind him, rending the air with their adulatory cries.

Throughout many days I remained in Zemnou. Once I saw the mysterious visitant pass in the darkness, and truly his luminous face shone like a lamp. One morning, however, while wandering among the palms outside the town, I met the Ruler of Earth walking alone, his head sunk upon his breast in pensive attitude. With his red cloak trailing heedlessly in the dust, he presented a decidedly dejected appearance. My footsteps startled him, and, raising his head quickly, he walked erect with his usual gait, apparently being desirous of concealing his melancholy.

"Praise!" I exclaimed, stopping, and bowing low before him. "If thou art, indeed, Allah, thou alone knowest the innermost thoughts of thy servant."

He paused, and stretched both his white tapering hands above my bowed head.

"Thy thoughts are of me," he answered. "Thou desirest speech with me alone. Speak."

So calmly he looked upon me that I was convinced that such a kindly, sympathetic face, with its expression of a sweet sadness, could not be human. Besides, had he not healed the sick, and caused trees to grow from out the desert sand? Yet a spirit of scepticism possessed me, and, scarcely knowing what words I uttered, I said—

"If thou art the mighty and wise One thou canst tell me my name, and whence I have come."

In an instant his brows knit, and his eyes flashed angrily.

"Thou art an unbeliever, and one of my accursed. Thou, who darest to question my immutability and omnipotence, go dwell with Eblis, Ruler of Darkness, where maleficent spirits shall haunt thee, and the tortures of the flesh shall rend thee for ever. Begone!"

And drawing his robe about his shoulders, he moved forward with truly imperial gait.

At that moment I saw through the trees a pious fanatical crowd approaching. The news had evidently spread that the All-merciful was walking in the outskirts of the town, and they had come forth to touch his garments and receive his blessing. But when he saw them he halted, and, pointing towards me, cried—

"Lo! Yonder is one of the sons of Eblis, a scoffer and unbeliever. Let his body be given to the dogs."

Ere I could realise that the kind-faced man had condemned me to death, the mob, with loud yells of execration, rushed forward to seize me, and hurry me to an ignominious end. But in an instant I dashed in among the trees, and fled for life so quickly that I at length managed to out-distance my irate pursuers, and till evening I slept beneath the shadow of a rock. Then, determined to speak again with the Almighty One, I returned into the town, taking the precaution to purchase new garments to prevent recognition.

The All-powerful had aroused further suspicion within me by his embarrassment when I had questioned him, and by his anxiety that I should be killed ere I could utter denunciation. Without doubt, he possessed a mixture of firmness and independence which raised him above all prejudices, for he expressed his opinions to Abreha, the Sheikh, with the same frankness he employed towards the humblest tribesman; nevertheless, when we had spoken, I had detected a dramatic pose and an artificiality of manner which puzzled me. Again, at the moment when I had addressed him, I had noticed, walking at some little distance behind him, a young girl of extreme beauty. She was unveiled, in the manner of the Kel-Alkoum, but somehow her face struck me as familiar, and I desired to again behold her. With that object I resumed my former quarters in the market-place, and kept watchful vigil. Next morning she came. Her face was paler than before, and it wore an anxious, terrified expression. I inquired who she was, and was told that to all she was a mystery. Whence she came no man knew, but Allah had declared her to be one of his chosen, hence none molested her, or made enquiry.

I smiled, for I had recognised her. She was Mezouda, daughter of one of our fighting men, who had been long ago captured by the Kel-Oui, and whose whereabouts had remained unknown.

An hour later I contrived to have secret speech with her. At first she did not recognise me, but when I told her who I was, then she at once expressed her eagerness to return to her own people.

"Thou shalt return to our camp only on one condition, namely, that thou wilt induce that man known as Allah to accompany thee," I answered. "He is thy friend."

"But the Kel-Alkoum are his well-beloved," she said, using the same expression he so often used.

"He must forsake them," I observed, explaining to her the baneful effect the report had exercised upon our men of the Azjar.

But she shook her head. "No, he will not leave the Kel-Alkoum. He is already their ruler," she said. "The power of Abreha is now fast waning."

"Take me to him," I commanded.

"But his house is a holy place. None dare enter on penalty of being cast out for ever."

"I will risk it," I answered. "Guide thither my footsteps."

Reluctantly she led me through a number of narrow crooked streets, until she paused before a small mud-built hut, and pointed to it.

Without ceremony I pushed open its closed door, and, entering, discerned the great King, half-dressed, standing before a scrap of broken mirror combing his beard. His face and neck were brown, so were his hands, but his breast and arms were white! The sympathetic countenance and tapering fingers were ingeniously stained to match the colour of the men of the desert, but the remainder of his body showed him to be a European.

"How darest thou thus disturb my privacy, accursed son of Eblis?" he cried in anger, evidently recognising me as the one whom he had condemned to death on the previous day.

"I have entered in order to denounce thy profane chicanery," I answered boldly. "Thou, the self-styled Allah, art an infidel, an impostor, and a fraud!"

He started at my fierce declaration, for the first time recollecting that parts of his chest, arms, and legs were exposed to my gaze. His face blanched beneath its artificial colouring, and his white lips trembled.

"Well!" he gasped, "and if thou hast discovered my secret—what then?"

"The people of the Kel-Alkoum shall be made aware of how completely they have been tricked," I answered, taking up a small pot, which I smelt, and found contained a preparation of phosphorous. This he had evidently used to cause his face to be luminous in the darkness.

"No!" he cried, "anything but that. I would rather kill myself outright than face the ferocity of these people."

"Then truthfully answer my questions," I said firmly, when I had explained to him who I was, and the sensation caused in our camp by the report of his assistance to our enemies. "Whence comest thou?"

"I come from the land of the Roumis over the great black water," he answered, suddenly casting off all cant and concealment. "My name is Mostyn Day, and I am an English mining prospector. Long ago, while in my own country, I read of the ease with which the fanatical Arabs may be imposed upon by fearless and unscrupulous men who desire to obtain power over them; and, truth to tell, hearing that great mineral wealth existed in the country of the Kel-Alkoum, and knowing Arabic well, I conceived a plan to come here, announce myself as Allah, and obtain over the tribe such complete authority and control that I should either become their Sheikh or obtain a concession to exploit all the mines in this rich region. My object was very nearly accomplished. To-morrow there is arranged a great rising of the people against Abreha, with the object of declaring me their ruler, but,"—and he paused sighing—"your discovery has put an end to it all."

"But what of the miracles you have worked in various villages?"

"Mere conjuring tricks and sleight-of-hand," he laughed. "Once, long ago, I was connected with an English travelling show, therefore I am familiar with most stage tricks. But now I have confessed to you, you will not expose me. Remember, unless you allow me to fly, these people will assuredly take my life."

"I will preserve silence on one condition only," I replied. "That to-night, an hour after sundown, you leave with me, journey to my encampment, and there exhibit to my people your painted face and arms, explaining to them the reason of your imposture, and showing them how you contrived to render your countenance luminous at night."

At first he demurred, but finding me inexorable he at length submitted, and asked to be allowed to take Mezouda with him.

"She is my wife," he explained. "I married her in Algiers two years ago, and by her aid alone have I been enabled to approach so nearly the realisation of the plot I had conceived."

"It was truly an ingenious one," I laughed. "Yes, Mezouda shall go with thee. Remain in silence of thine intentions, and meet me among the palms outside the town an hour after sundown."

At first I feared that the intrepid Englishman, who had so nearly been the cause of a great Jehad through the whole Sahara, would endeavour to escape, but both he and his pretty and adventurous wife kept the appointment, and after some days we eventually arrived at our encampment.

The excitement caused by our appearance was unbounded. Taghma and his companions at once recognised the Englishman in his blood-red robe as the Allah of the Kel-Alkoum, and all fell on their knees, crying aloud in adoration.

But their supplications were quickly cut short by the few loud words of authority I uttered, and when half an hour later the reckless adventurer exhibited his stained face and hands, and then entertained them by showing the simple means by which he accomplished his tricks of magic, the air was rent by roars of laughter. The veiled warriors of the Azjar danced for joy, and held their sides when convinced how completely their enemies had been tricked, and how dejected they, no doubt, were when they knew that the Allah, in whom they trusted, had forsaken them without a single word of farewell.

For a month the ingenious impostor remained a guest within our tents; then he departed for the north, taking his wife Mezouda with him. But since that day the Kel-Alkoum, believing themselves the forgotten of Allah, have ever been a cowed and peaceful nation.

Chapter Six.

The Evil of the Thousand Eyes.

The camp fire was dying in the gloomy hour before the dawn. In the Great Desert the light comes early from the far-off Holy City, golden as the Prophet's glory, to light our footsteps in those trackless waterless wastes which are shunned by man and forgotten by Allah. My tribesmen of the Azjar, still wrapped in their black veils, were sleeping soundly prior to the long march of the coming day, and all was quiet save the howling of a desert fox, and the shuffling tread of the sentries as they traversed the camp from end to end, silent and weird in their long black burnouses and veils. Alone, I was sitting gazing into the dying embers, deep in thought. I had been unable to sleep, for a strange premonition of danger oppressed me. We were in the country of the Taïtok, a tribe of pure Arabs, fierce in battle, who when united with the Kel-Rhela, their neighbours, were among our most formidable opponents. The Sheikhs of both tribes had made treaty with the French, and placed their country beneath the protection of the tricolour of the Infidels, therefore in our expedition, against their town of Azal, we knew that we must meet with considerable opposition.

We had exercised every caution in our advance, travelling by various ancient dried-up watercourses known only to us, "The Breath of the Wind," approaching in secret the town we intended to loot and burn as a reprisal for an attack made upon us a month before. But the report of a spy, who had gone forward to Azal, was exceedingly discouraging. The French had occupied the Kasbah, the red-burnoused Spahis were swaggering about the streets and market-places, while the tricolour floated over the city gate, and the fierce fighting men of the Taïtok were now fearless of any invader. It was this report which caused me considerable uneasiness, and I was calmly reflecting whether to turn off to the east into the barren Ahaggar, or to push forward and measure our strength with our enemies, the Infidels, when suddenly my eyes, sharpened by a lifetime of desert wandering, detected a dark crouching figure moving in the gloom at a little distance from me. In an instant I snatched up my rifle and covered it. Unconscious of how near death was, the mysterious stranger still moved slowly across, lying upon his stomach and dragging himself along the sand in the direction of my tent. As I looked, a slight flash caught my eye. It was the gleam of the flickering flame upon burnished steel. The man held a knife, and at the door of my tent raised himself before entering, then disappeared within.

Quick as thought I jumped up, drew my keen double-edged *jambiyah* from my girdle, and noiselessly sped towards my tent, drawing aside the flap, and dashing in to capture the intruder.

The dark figure was bending over a portfolio wherein I keep certain writings belonging to the tribe, the compacts of friends and the threats of foes.

"Thou art my prisoner!" I cried fiercely, halting inside, casting aside my knife and raising my rifle.

The figure turned quickly with a slight scream, and by the feeble light of my hanging-lamp I was amazed to detect the features of a woman, young, beautiful, with a face almost as white as those of the Roumi women who sit at cafés in Algiers.

"Mercy, O Ahamadou!" she implored, next second casting herself upon her knees before me. "True, I have fallen prisoner into thine hands, but the Book of Everlasting Will declares that thou shalt neither hold in slavery nor kill those who art thy friends. I crave thy mercy, for indeed I am thy friend."

"Yet thou seekest my life with that knife in thine hand!" I cried in anger. "Whence comest thou?" I demanded, for her Arabic was a dialect entirely strange to me.

"From a country afar—a region which no man knoweth," she answered.

"The country of the Azjar is the whole of the Great Desert," I answered, with pride. "Every rock and every wady is known unto them."

"Not every wady," she replied, smiling mysteriously. "They know not the Land of Akkar, nor the City of the Golden Tombs."

"The Land of Akkar!" I gasped, for Akkar was a region which only existed in the legendary lore of the Bedouins, and was supposed to be a fabulous country, wherein lived a mysterious race of white people, and where was concealed the enormous treasure captured during the Mussulman Conquest. "Knowest thou actually the position of the wondrous Land of Akkar?"

"It is my home," she answered in soft sibillation, as stretching forth my hand I motioned her to rise. I saw that her beauty and grace were perfect. She wore no veil, but her dark robe was dusty and stained by long travel, while her striking beauty was enhanced by a string of cut emeralds of great size and lustre across her brow, in place of the sequins with which our women decorate themselves. She wore no other jewels, save a single diamond upon the index-finger of the right hand, a stone of wondrous size and brilliancy. It seemed to gleam like some monster eye as she sank upon the divan near, a slight sigh of fatigue escaping her.

"And thy name?" I enquired.

"Nara, daughter of Kiagor," she answered. "And thou art the great Ahamadou, whom all men fear from Lake Tsâd, even unto the confines of Algeria, the leader of the dreaded Breath of the Wind. In our secret land reports of thy prowess and ferocity in the fight, of thy leniency towards the women and children of thine enemies, have already reached us, therefore I travelled alone to seek thee."

And she looked up into my face, her full red lips parted in a smile.

"Why?" I enquired, puzzled.

"Because I crave the protection of thine host of black-veiled warriors," she answered. "Our land of Akkar is threatened by an invasion of the Infidel English, who have sent two spies northward from the Niger. May Allah burn their vitals! They succeeded in penetrating into our mountain fastness, and were captured by our scouts. One was killed, but the other escaped. He has, undoubtedly, gone back to his own people; and they will advance upon us, for they are a nation the most powerful and most fearless in all the world."

"Of a verity thy lips utter truth," I observed, "for we once fought in the Dervish ranks against the English on the Nile bank, and were cut down like sun-dried grass before the scythe. But who hath sent thee as messenger to me?"

"I come on my own behalf," she responded. "I am ruler of the Akkar."

It was strange, sitting there in conversation with the ruler of a mysterious region, the existence of which every Arab in the Soudan and the Sahara firmly believed, yet no man had ever set foot in the legendary country, the fabulous wealth and strange sights of which were related by every story-teller from Khartoum even unto Timbuktu. And yet Nara, the Queen of Akkar, was a guest within my camp, and had fallen upon her knees before me in supplication. Ambition was fired within me to visit her wondrous land of the silent dead, and I announced my readiness to effect a treaty with her, first accompanying her alone to see the wonders of her mystic realm. As I spoke, however, a curious change appeared to come over her. Her face flushed slightly, her eyes gleamed with a fiery glance, and there was a hardness about her mouth, which, for one brief moment, caused me suspicion.

"Thou art welcome, O Ahamadou!" she answered, smiling bewitchingly, next instant. "We will start even now, if thou wilt, for no time must be lost ere thine armed men unite with the guards of my kingdom to resist the accursed English, that white-faced tribe whom Eblis hath marked as his own. Let us speed on the wings of haste, and within a week thou mayest be back here within thine own camp."

And she rose in readiness to go forth.

"My *meheri* is tethered behind yon rock," she continued, pointing out beyond the camp where a great dark rock loomed forth against the fast-clearing sky. "Join me there, and I will guide thy footsteps unto my City of the Golden Tombs."

Whilst she went forth secretly I called Malela, son of Tamahu, and imparted to him the circumstances, telling him of my intention to go secretly to Akkar, and giving him instructions how to preserve from the tribe the fact that I was absent. Malela was one of the fiercest of desert-pirates, as valiant a man as ever drew a *jambiyah* against an enemy; but when I mentioned my intended visit to the silent legendary land, the wealth and terrors of which he had heard hundreds of times from the lips of the story-tellers and marabouts, his face paled beneath its bronze.

"May the One of Praise envelope thee with the cloak of His protection," he ejaculated with heartfelt fervency. "Have we not heard of the awful tortures of those in the mute land—the mysterious region which the Moors have declared to be the veritable dwelling-place of Eblis, the region inhabited by those who have served the Devil and refused both the blessings of Allah and the intercessions of his Prophet?"

"Are not the Azjar without fear, and is not Ahamadou their leader?" I asked proudly, reflecting upon Nara's marvellous beauty, and feeling an intense curiosity to visit the country wherein no man had hitherto set foot. Again, had not the Queen of Akkar singled out the Veiled Men of the Azjar as her allies against the eaters of unclean meat, the Infidels whose bodies Allah will burn with his all-consuming fire.

Again Malela uttered a prayer to the One, as he stood facing the Holy Ca'aba, and I, too, murmured a *sûra* as I thrust some cartridges into my pouch, drew tighter my belt with its amulets sewn within, and buckled on my sword with the wondrous jewel in the hilt—the mark of chieftainship—for I was to be guest of the Queen of an unknown land.

Then, with a whispered farewell to Tamahu's son, I stole forth, treading softly among my sleeping tribesmen, and carefully avoiding the sentries until I came to my own swift camel, I mounted it, and a few minutes later joined my handsome guide. She had already mounted, and had twisted a white haick about her face until only her eyes and the row of emeralds across her brow remained visible.

It is needless to recount the long breathless days we spent together in journeying westward, resting by day and travelling ever in the track of the blood-red afterglow, until we came upon a range of giant snow-crested mountains, as great as the monster Atlas that loom as a barrier between ourselves and the so-called civilisation of the Franks.

"Yonder," she said, pointing to them, when first their grandeur burst upon our view in the pale rose of dawn. "Yonder is our land which none can enter, save those who know the secret way. There are but two entrances—one here and the other far south, the way through which the English have unfortunately discovered."

"Then on all sides but one thy kingdom is impregnable," I observed, gazing with amazement at the serrated barrier, which seemed to rise until it reached the misty cloud-land.

"On all but one," she answered. "Those who know not the secret must meet with death, because of the dangers by which Akkar is surrounded as safeguards against her enemies."

Throughout two days we travelled, slowly approaching the snowy range, and one night we halted beside a narrow lake, beyond which was practically an impassable barrier of rugged cliffs and towering mountains. The night was moonless, and as I laid down to sleep, only the rippling of the water lapping the pebbles broke the appalling stillness. At last, however, I dropped off into a heavy slumber, and was only awakened by a strange roar in my ears like the thunder of a cataract.

I put forth my hand and tried to open my eyes, but both efforts were alike useless. To my amazement I found my hands secured behind me, and my eyes blindfolded.

Then, in an instant, it occurred to me that I had been entrapped. I struggled and fought to free myself, for the air was hot and stifling, and I felt myself being asphyxiated with a deadening roar in my ears, and a close indescribable odour in my nostrils. In my attempt to tear the irritating bandage from my eyes, my head came suddenly into contact with something soft. I placed my cheek against it, and found to my amazement that I was lying on some kind of silken divan, my head supported by an embroidered cushion of the kind usual in our harems.

But the odour about me was not the intoxicating fragrance of burning pastilles, but a damp mouldy smell, as of a chamber long closed.

How long my mental torture and sense of utter helplessness continued I know not. All I recollect is that, of a sudden, the air seemed fresher and cooler, the thunder of the waters died away instantly, and the smell of the charnel-house gave place to a delicate perfume of fresh flowers. There was a genial warmth upon my cheeks, and I awakened to the fact that the sun was shining upon me, when I felt a hand unloosen the bandage tied behind my head, and heard the voice of Nara say—

"Lo, the danger is past. Thou art in Akkar," and she drew away the piece of black folded silk that had held me without vision.

In abject amazement I looked around stupefied. We were together in a kind of boat shaped like an inverted funnel, which opened only at the top and could be closed at will by a complicated arrangement of levers and wire ropes, a subaquatic vessel fitted with comfortable lounges, having a lighted lamp hanging in the centre. Everything—seats, tables, and all the fittings—swung in rings, therefore, whichever way the boat rolled, even though it might turn complete somersaults, those riding in it could remain seated without inconvenience. On looking back I saw that the narrow stream we were navigating was fed by a mighty torrent that rushed from the mountain-side, a roaring, boiling flood which sent up a great column of spray, reflecting in the sunlight all the colours of the spectrum; and I also observed that we had entered the Land of Akkar by means of that strangely-shaped boat of bolted iron plates as strong as the war-ships of the Infidels, and were now in a deep and fertile valley, having descended from the lake by an unknown subterranean watercourse through the very heart of the giant mountain.

I gazed about me in blank amazement, for even as my conductress spoke, she deftly stretched forth a pole and arrested the progress of the boat at a flight of well-worn steps, while above, my wondering eyes fell upon the great white façade of a palace with an enormous gilded dome.

"Yonder is my dwelling-place," she explained with a wave of the hand, and as we stepped upon the bank a crowd of fierce-looking armed warriors appeared, raising their spears high in salutation.

"This is Ahamadou," she explained, "the dreaded Sheikh of the Azjar, who hath come to make brotherhood with us. He is guest of Nara, thy Ruler."

"Welcome, O Ahamadou!" they cried, with one voice. "Of a verity thou art the lion of the desert, for the leader of the Breath of the Wind knoweth not fear."

"I am thy friend, O friends," I answered, as by Nara's side I strode onward to the wondrous palace, so magnificent, yet of such delicate architecture that one marvelled how human hands could have fashioned it. The country I had entered was red with flowers and green with many leaves; a fruitful, peaceful region, the spires and domes of the great City of the Golden Tombs rising in the distance far down the valley, white and clear-cut as cameos against the liquid gold of the sunset.

Together we ascended the long flight of marble steps which led to the great colonnade, and gave entrance to a palace of similar design to those of the ancient palaces of Egypt in those forgotten days long before the Prophet. As our feet touched the last step, the air was rent by a fanfare of a hundred trumpets, causing the valley to re-echo. Then a file of armed men, headed by the blood-red banner of Akkar, lined our route, bowing low as we passed on into a hall, high vaulted and of enormous proportions, in the centre of which stood a wonderful throne of gold, covered with hundreds upon hundreds of eyes of every variety and size, wrought in gems to imitate those of human beings and of animals. As I gazed upon it I suddenly recollected what I had heard from the story-tellers about this wondrous seat of Akkar's Queen. It was the ancient throne whereon, for nearly two thousand years, the rulers of the City of the Golden Tombs had sat, and was known in legendary lore as the Throne of the Thousand Eyes, each eye recording a battle, and being formed of the greatest gem taken in the loot on that occasion. As I approached I saw that some were of diamonds, others of rubies, of emeralds, of jade, of jacinth, of jasper, of pearl, and of sapphires, each perfectly formed, but some kindly-looking, while on others the expression was that of terror, of hatred, or of agony, truly the strangest and weirdest seat of royalty in all the world.

Around me the excitement rose to fever-heat as the people assembled, and Nara seated herself upon the throne after casting aside the travel-stained haick she had worn on the journey. I saw everywhere evidences of unbounded riches. The silken robes of the courtiers were sewn with jewels, and as their queen sank among her soft cushions, and her women put upon her necklaces and anklets of enormous worth, the great chamber became filled with the clank of arms and the murmur of many voices, while I was closely scrutinised and my appearance commented upon. Suddenly, the great Queen rose, lifting her arms, and with an expression of uncontrollable anger upon her white face, said—

"Lo, my people, hear this my word! I have travelled afar into the country of our enemies, and have brought hither the person of Ahamadou, their chief."

"I am not thine enemy, O Queen!" I hastened to assure her. "Thine ally, if thou wilt."

"I have brought hither this man," she cried, "I have brought him hither in fulfilment of my oath in order that punishment shall be meted out to him."

"Punishment!" I gasped, wondering if I had taken leave of my senses.

"Remember, that this man is Ahamadou, chief of the pirates, who have captured so many of our caravans, and who slew my son Kourra, heir to this my throne, six moons ago!" she cried, in a paroxysm of rage, lifting her thin bare arms, her face growing hideous in her fearful ebullition of anger. I saw that I had fallen helplessly into the hands of my enemies, and bit my lip without uttering a single word. To escape from that unexplored rock-bound kingdom was hopeless. I could only show them that fear dwelleth not in the heart of an Azjar, even though thousands lifted their hands against him.

"I have," she cried, "sought out this man, alone and unaided, according to the oath I took before the sacred scarabaeus upon this the Throne of the Thousand Eyes, and conducted him hither in order that ye may pass judgment upon him. Speak, say what torture shall he undergo?"

In an instant the air was rent by loud cries of—

"Let the scarabaeus devour him! Let him witness the torture of the spies, and afterwards let the same be applied to him! Let him die the most terrible of all deaths; let the sacred beetle crush him beneath its fangs!"

A dozen men, aged, white-robed, with beards so long that some almost swept the ground, whom I judged were priests, held brief consultation: then, amid the uproar, they seized me, wrenched from me my arms, and led me away ere I could raise my voice to charge their dreaded ruler with treachery. Followed by the jeering, excited multitude, they conducted me along the wide level road to the mysterious city, upon the high gates of which were mounted strong guards, with breast-plates whereon the image of the sacred beetle was worked in crimson, and through great streets and squares until we came to a huge mosquelike structure, the three golden domes of which I had noticed glittering afar as the dying rays of the sunset slanted upon them.

The dimly-lit interior was magnificent, but as they dragged me forward, I saw placed beneath the central dome a colossal figure of the sacred Scarabaeus a hundred feet in height, and two hundred feet square, plated over with gold. From the two hideous eyes shone lines of white light like the rays of the searchlights of the Infidels, while, by some mechanical contrivance, the wide mouth now and then opened and closed, as though the monstrous emblem of the eternal were eager to devour those who worshipped before it.

The bearded priests who held me threw themselves upon their knees before it in adoration, uttering a low kind of chant, while almost at the same instant a quivering terrified man, haggard, thin, and bearing signs of long imprisonment, was dragged forth from a kind of cell in the colossal walls, and made to bend upon his knees upon a grey circular stone immediately before the monster Throat of Death.

"No! no!" he shrieked in horror. "Kill me by the sword! Let my body be given to the alligators—anything—but spare me the torture of the Beetle! I am innocent! It is but Nara's love of bloodshed and torture of the flesh that hath caused her to condemn me. May the curse of the Beetle be ever upon her!"

Ere he could utter another word six black slaves, veritable giants in stature, seized the unfortunate wretch, and as the mouth of the monster again opened, they flung him headlong into it.

Next second the cruel terrible mouth closed, and the shrieks and crushing of bones told how terrible was the torture of the human victim within its insatiable maw.

The sight caused me to shudder. To this frightful ignominious death had this fair-faced, soft-spoken woman condemned me.

Again the enormous golden jaws opened, and again, as they closed, the victim's piercing shrieks told that his agony was renewed, and that death did not come quickly within that weird colossal figure of the insect, once held sacred from the shores of the Red Sea unto the great black ocean. In this, the last place in all the world where its worship still remained, the people were the most cruel and relentless of any in our great dark continent, Africa. A dozen times the mouth opened and closed, and each occasion the cries of the agonised man were frightful to hear, until at last they died away, and as they did so the light also died from the monster's eyes.

Soon, however, another thin, cringing man, starved almost to a skeleton, was brought forth, and with similar scant ceremony was cast into the colossal jaws, whereupon the light in the giant eyes grew brilliant again, and the shrieks for release, as the mouth reopened, were only answered by the loud jeers of the assembled multitude, by this time increased until every part of the magnificent building was crowded to suffocation, while at that instant Nara, still upon the Throne of the

Thousand Eyes, was dragged in by a crowd of nearly a thousand persons. Twelve black slaves slowly fanned her as she sat, her chin resting upon her hand, watching in silence.

One after another were victims brought forth and hurled to the horrible monster, to be slowly cut to pieces by the myriad gleaming knives and fine-edged saws set within those terrible jaws, until at last some one in the crowd cried out with a loud voice—

"Let the pirate Ahamadou die! His men killed our Prince, the valiant Kourra, therefore no mercy shall be shown the Veiled Man. Let him be given to the Sacred Beetle!"

In an instant the cry was taken up on every hand. "Let him die!" they shouted wildly. "Let us witness his body being cut to ribbons!"

The priests hesitated, while in that perilous moment I repeated a *sûra*, and heeded not these Infidel worshippers of insects and idolators of golden effigies.

But at a sign from Nara, the relentless figure in white seated upon her wondrous Throne of the Thousand Eyes, they seized me, forced me to kneel upon the circular stone, and then, as those hideous jaws opened with a swift movement, they lifted me and cast me in.

For an instant my head reeled, and all breath left me, for I knew that a fearful agonising death was nigh; but as Allah willed it, I alighted upon my feet, and finding in the darkness that the floor sloped down, I started running with all my might, gashing myself upon the knives, set upright like teeth, but nevertheless speedily forward, heedless of the pain. Slowly and surely the walls of that strange torture-chamber closed about me with a creaking and groaning horrible to hear, until I found myself squeezed tightly with irresistible force on every side. I held my breath, for upon my chest was a great weight, and I knew that next instant my frame must be crushed to pulp.

Slowly, however, almost imperceptibly, the frightful pressure upon my body began to relax, and ere I realised the welcome truth, I found myself able to breathe again. By dashing forward I had advanced far down the dreaded Throat of Death to a point where the passage began to widen, and by the freshness of the air I now felt that some outlet lay beyond. Therefore, without hesitation, I sped again onward, stumbling over some soft objects on the ground, which I instinctively knew to be the remains of my fellow victims, until a faint grey glimmer of light showed in the distance. The floor still sloped steeply, and by feeling about me, I discovered that the Throat was now simply a natural burrow in the rock.

Without loss of a second I soon gained the outlet, and peered forth, aghast to discover that the tunnel ended abruptly in the face of a bare precipice; and that in the valley some two hundred feet below lay a great heap of sun-bleached bones, the remains of those who had passed through the Throat of Death. Undoubtedly, when the channel became choked with the rotting remains of the victims they were cast forth to the vultures and the wolves.

Eager to escape from the noisome place, I climbed with difficulty down the face of the mountain, and on gaining the valley, quickly recognised, with satisfaction, that I was actually beyond the confines of the accursed Land of Akkar. Truly I had encountered death as a very near neighbour. The high range with their snowy crests were the same as my treacherous guide had pointed out to me, and next day I skirted the lake which, emptying itself by the subterranean river, gave entrance to the mystic land of Nara. Through many weary weeks I travelled hither and thither, ill and half-starved, until at length I fell in with a camel caravan, and travelling with them to Idelès, subsequently rejoined my own tribesmen, who had, by that time, begun to despair of my safety.

Within six moons I made a report of the mysterious land, and all that I had witnessed therein, to the Bureau Arabe, in Algiers, and ere six more moons had waned, the Franks sent an armed expedition to enter and explore the country. Of this expedition I was appointed guide, all past offences of my tribesmen being forgiven; but the soldiers of Nara offering a determined resistance, their country was at once subdued and occupied by the white conquerors. The sacred Scarabaeus was destroyed by dynamite, and the Throat of Death widened until it now forms one of the entrances to the land so long unknown. The dreaded Nara was sent as prisoner down to Senegal, where she still lives in exile; but her wondrous throne still remains in her great white palace—now a barrack of the Spahis and Chasseurs—and the Arab story-tellers in every desert town, from the Atlas to Lake Tsâd, continue to relate weird and wonderful tales of the City of the Golden Tombs and the Evil of the Thousand Eyes.

Chapter Seven.

The Gate of Hell.

Lounging on a bench under the tall date-palms in the market-place of Hamman-el-Enf, I smoked a rank *cherbli* in dreamy laziness. The day was dying; the blazing African sun sank, flooding the broad Bay of Tunis with its blood-red afterglow, and the giant palms cast their long, straight shadows over the hot, sun-blanched stones. There are no half lights in Northern Africa; all is either glaring brilliance or sombre shadow. Little twilight is there in that land of mosques and marabouts; night follows the death of day with astonishing rapidity. Even while I sat, darkness crept on; the squatting, chattering crowd of white-burnoused Moors and Arabs and red-fezzed negroes had dispersed, and the sunbaked little village seemed almost deserted. Suddenly the white figure of an Arab woman glided slowly and ghost-like from the deep shadow of the ilexes. Like all others of her sex, she was enshrouded in a *haick*, and the lower portion of her face was hidden by her thick white veil, only a magnificent pair of black sparkling eyes, and a forehead upon which rows of gold sequins tinkled, being visible.

Halting for a few seconds, she stared at me as if in surprise, then, in soft musical Arabic, gave me peace, exclaiming—

"Sadness dwelleth in the heart of the Touareg. Of a verity thou art not more sad than I," and, sighing, she drew her *adjar* closer across her face, and was about to pass on.

"Sad, art thou?" I answered, surprised that she should address me, a veiled man of the desert. In the dim light I could distinguish that her hose were of the finest white silk, that her tiny shoes were Paris made and of patent leather, and that the hand which held the *haick* around her was loaded with valuable rings. "Loosen thy tongue's strings, O one of beauty," I said, gallantly. "Tell me why speakest thou unto me; why unhappiness hath fallen upon thee."

"Ah, no!" she replied, in a hoarse half-whisper, glancing round in apparent fear. "My people must not observe me having speech with thee. Ah, Allah may bring one of us to Certainty before to-morrow, and—if thou wouldst only help me!"

"What service can I render?" I asked, quickly, well aware that the fact of her speaking to a Touareg in a public place was of itself a very grave offence in the eyes of the fanatical Aïssâwa. The barrier between the Berber and the Touareg in Tunis is still insurmountable.

"First, thou must trust me," she said frankly. "I am called Fathma Khadidja; and thy name—already I know it. It is dangerous for me to hold converse here with thee. Let thy footsteps follow mine. Come, and may Allah, who knoweth the innermost parts of the breasts of men, shower upon thee bounteous blessings," and she turned and started off with that waddling gait peculiar to all Arab women.

I hesitated. If really in distress, it was strange that she had not called upon her own people to help her, instead of requesting a Touareg and a stranger to render assistance.

No. I decided not to go, and sat watching her receding figure cross the market-place where slaves were sold even within recent years, and disappear in the shadow of the mosque.

In an hour I had forgotten the mysterious Fathma and her troubles, and returned to Tunis.

Next afternoon, as I entered my temporary abode in the Kasbah-Kasneh, my slave handed me a note. As I tore it open it emitted an odour of geranium, the favourite perfume of the harem. Having read the three long lines of sprawly Arabic characters it contained, I placed the missive in my pocket and turned away. If I valued my life, I was to meet Khadidja that evening. Was that a threat, or a warning? During the remainder of that day I lounged outside the cafés and pondered deeply. For hours I ruminated over absinthe and mazagran, cassis and bock; and, after much consideration, I at length resolved to keep the appointment, and ascertain the extent of the mysterious danger of which she wrote.

At the appointed hour I awaited her at a secluded spot outside the Bab Alewa. The clock of the Mosque of Sidi Mahrez, close by, struck solemnly, and as the last sound died away I heard the *frou-frou* of feminine garments, as a shrouded figure advanced to meet me.

"Ah, so thou hast kept thine appointment, O Touareg!" she exclaimed, stretching forth to me a soft white hand. "Thou thinkest, because I believe in the One, and in Mahomet his Prophet, that I am unworthy thy regard; that I am not to be trusted, eh?" Then she laughed lightly, adding, "Come, let us hasten. I want to have serious speech with thee upon a matter that affecteth us both."

Without replying, I walked on beside her, wondering whether she were ugly or beautiful. Crossing a deserted garden, we passed out to where two asses were tethered, and, mounting them, rode away into the darkness. I remember that we went through several villages, and at length came to a larger place built upon the low cliffs, where a number of spacious flat-roofed houses overlooked the sea.

Suddenly she dismounted before a low arched door in one of the great square, inartistic, whitewashed residences, and placed her fingers upon her lips indicative of silence. Taking a key that was suspended around her neck, she unlocked the door and led me into a dark passage so thickly carpeted that my feet fell noiselessly as she guided me onward. Once I caught a glimpse of a spacious patio, rendered cool by a plashing fountain and green with many leaves; then through two small chambers we passed, until we came to a closed door, which she opened, and I found myself in a spacious, dimly illumined apartment, decorated in quaint Arabesques of dark crimson and dull gold. Everything was rich and luxurious. The air was heavy with sensuous odours rising in a thin blue column from the gold perfuming-pan. On the floor lay costly Arab rugs, and a couple of lion skins were thrown down on each side of the centre mat. A *derbouka*, and a *ginkri*, fashioned from a tortoise-shell, lay thrown aside, while from a magnificent hanging-lamp of gold a soft, mellow light was diffused, though scarcely sufficient to show the heavy draperies that concealed the walls.

"Best thee a moment, and I will return," my mysterious veiled guide said; and then, drawing aside some of the silken hangings, she disappeared through a door that had been hidden.

With hands behind me, I slowly wandered round, wondering what apartment of the house this was, when some half-finished embroidery that had apparently been tossed hurriedly aside upon a coffee stool of inlaid pearl and silver caught my eye. That told me the truth. My heart gave a sudden bound. I was in the harem!

A French novel lay open on one of the little tables. I took it up, and, as I stood in wonderment, a movement behind me caused me to turn, and then I beheld the most beautiful woman I had ever gazed upon. She was not more than twenty-two, with a complexion fresh as a Frenchwoman's, features that were perfect, pretty lips parted in a glad smile, and a dress that was the most gorgeous I had ever seen. The ugly *haick* had been replaced by a *rlila* of palest leaf-green brocaded silk, beneath which showed a rose-pink velvet vest; and, in the place of the baggy trousers, she wore the *serroual*, of silken gauze. Her tiny bare feet were thrust into slippers of rose velvet; on her head was set jauntily a little crimson skull-cap embroidered with seed-pearls; and her *fouta*, or sash, was of tricolour-striped silk, richly ornamented with gold. Upon her bare arms and ankles diamonds flashed and sparkled with a thousand fires, and her bangles jingled as she moved. She dazzled and fascinated me.

With an apology for having left me, she sank slowly among her cushions with graceful abandon, at the same time losing one of her slippers, and motioning me to a seat near her.

"Thou thinkest it strange," she said; "perhaps even thou art angry, that I have brought thee hither alone unto this gilded cage. But I must speak with thee, O Man of the Desert—to warn thee;" and her dimpled chin rested upon her dainty palm as she, with seriousness, looked straight into my eyes.

"To warn me! Of what?"

"Thou art threatened," she answered slowly. "Thou wilt, perhaps, remember that a month ago thou wert in Kabylia, and left Fort National for Tizi Ouzou. Thou hadst the careless indifference that thy free life giveth, and, no doubt, thou wert prepared to meet Eblis himself if he promised an adventure. On that occasion with whom didst thou travel?"

"I journeyed in company of a wealthy man of thy people, who was returning from the wine market."

"True, O friend," she replied. "A week ago thou didst describe that journey to a Frank of the *Moniteur de l'Algérie*, and ridiculed thy companion. See here!" and stretching forth her hand, she took up a paper containing an interview in which I had treated the journey in a comic vein, and had denounced in no measured terms the bigotry of my fellow-traveller.

"Thou art a Veiled Man; and that man," she continued, "hath sworn upon the book of Everlasting Will to kill thee!"

"How dost thou know this, O thou whose face is rivalled only by the sun?" I asked quickly.

"Because—because the man thou hast ridiculed is my husband!" she replied, rising, and adding wildly, "Because I overheard the villainous scheme that he hath planned with his brother to take thy life, and at the risk of mine own honour I determined to save thee. Allah alone knoweth how terrible is my life alone in this place with my servants, bound to a fierce, brutal man who loveth me not, and upon whose brow the Câfer hath set seal."

"Is thy husband neglectful, then?" I asked, noticing the poignant sorrow that in that moment seemed to have crushed her.

"Alas! yes. Whithersoever I go the curse of Sajin seemeth upon me," she sighed, passing her slim, bejewelled hand slowly across her white forehead. Tears welled in her brilliant eyes, as she added in a broken voice, "I am lost—lost to all; soulless, uncared for, unloved."

She hesitated a moment thoughtfully, glancing first at her own bejewelled hands find then at mine. With a quick movement she drew from one of her fingers a curious ring of silver, around which were Arabic characters in gold.

"See!" she cried, as if a sudden thought had occurred to her. "Take this, and wear it. It is my talisman, and as long as it is upon thy finger no harm can befall thee. It beareth the stamp of 'La Belle,' and will preserve thee in health and guard thee in the hour of tribulation."

She took my hand in hers, and drawing my own ring from my finger, replaced it by her strange-looking talisman, afterwards slipping my own ring upon her hand. A sob escaped her. "We have exchanged rings!" she exclaimed brokenly, looking up into my face with tear-stained, world-weary eyes. Then, clutching her bare breast as if to still the throbbing of her heart, she cried, "When—when thou art far away, thou wilt, peradventure, sometimes gaze upon mine, and remember that a service was once rendered thee by a poor, unhappy woman—thou wilt recollect that her name is Fathma Khadidja—that—that—ah! forgive me, for I am mad! mad!"

Raising my hand to her warm lips, she kissed it passionately with all the fire and ardour of the Child of the Sun. Then, releasing me, she tottered back, panting, and sank upon her silken divan, with her face buried in her hands, sobbing as if her heart would break.

"*Cama tafâkal kathalika tolâ ki,*" I said, quoting at random from the Korân. "Come, come," I added sympathetically, sinking down beside her, tenderly stroking her long, silky tresses. "Despair not. The One Worthy of Praise knoweth how thou sufferest, and will give unto thee strength in the hour of thy need, and bring thee into the shadow of the great lote tree."

"Ah! Thy mouth uttereth pearls of wisdom," she cried wildly. "But I have touched thee, a Touareg, and am accursed by Allah. I care nought for the future, for already am I forsaken, already have I tasted of the bitter fruit of Al-Zakkum, and am doomed to the torture of Al-Hâwiyat, the place prepared for the evil-doers." Then, raising her face to mine, with an intense look of passionate love, she said in a soft, sibilant whisper, "Once only! Kiss me once! Then thou mayest go, and never shall we meet—never!"

Her beautiful head fell upon my shoulder, and her hair—soft as spun silk—strayed across my face. For a moment her lips met mine in a hot, passionate kiss, a caress enough to make any man's head reel.

"I love thee," she whispered, in low, half-frightened tones, as she clung to me, and would not allow me to release myself. "Unseen by thee, I have watched thee many moons, and to-night have I brought thee hither to tell thee—to confess to thee my secret."

I tried to draw my lingering lips from hers, but with the fire of passion gleaming in her brilliant eyes she gripped me with a force I should not have supposed her capable of.

"Stay," she whispered. "Without thee the canker-worm of love eateth away my heart."

But I tore myself from her and left.

Next day my business of selling sheep took me to the Haras Fortress, away behind the hills of Ahmar, and the voices of the *muddenin* were already calling the faithful for the *maghrib* when I re-entered the Kasbah. Kasneh, my slave, was playing *damma* in the courtyard, but rose quietly, saluted, and told me that he had taken to my room a small package which had been left by the negro servant that had brought the letter on the previous day.

Could it, I wondered, be a present from Khadidja? Rushing in, I found on my table a small box, packed in white paper and secured with black seals. Eagerly I tore away the wrappings and opened it.

As I did so a shriek of horror escaped me. I fell back awe-stricken at the sight presented. Inside a satin-lined bracelet-case, bearing the name of a Paris jeweller, on a piece of pale-blue velvet, there was stretched a human finger that had been roughly hacked off at the joint! It lay stiff, white, and cold, with the blood coagulated where the blunt knife had jagged the flesh. The finger was a woman's—slim, well-formed, with the nail stained by henna. It was loaded with costly rings, which scintillated in the golden ray of sunset that strayed into the room, and fell across them. As I looked, breathless in amazement, I saw among the ornaments my own ring!

A scrap of paper that fluttered to the ground bore the words, scrawled in Arabic character, "From the husband of Fathma Khadidja!"

That same night I strode furiously along the seashore, watching the glimmering lights in the distance. In fear and trepidation, I took the hideous souvenir of love, and, when far from the city, cast it away from me into the dark rolling waters.

Perhaps there, deep in its lonely hiding-place, it met the white, dead thing of which it had once formed part—the body of the matchless daughter of the sun whose wondrous hair enmeshed me, whose full, red lips held me like a magnet, shackling me to the inevitable. Who can tell?

Truly, in that brief hour when I lounged at her side, I was at the dreaded Bab-el-Hâwiyat.

Chapter Eight.

The Queen of the Silent Kingdom.

I entered the Silent Kingdom six years ago.

Praise be to Allah, whom the weight of a pearl upon the earth does not escape. May prayer and salvation be with the master of the first and last, our Lord Mahommed. Of a verity have I been blessed with blessings abundant, and enveloped by the cloak of his protection.

We had left the shore of Lake Tsâd after pillaging a great caravan from the north, and were moving westward across the stern, sterile desert in the direction of Gao, or Kou-kou, as it is popularly known among us, where we could dispose of our stolen merchandise. For months we had travelled across that immensity of sands where the very birds lose themselves, our camels often stumbling upon some skull, tibia, or even an entire skeleton, the remains of bygone generations of travellers who had perished on those lonely wastes. The sun blazed fiercely in the flaming sky, the skin cracked, the lips were parched. All the water we had was warm and impure, and even that was insufficient to quench our thirst. A scaly viper occasionally crossed our route, and at long intervals the swift flight of an antelope was seen. For days, months, nothing had rejoiced our eyes save the deceitful vision of the mirage, and one evening I decided upon a three days' halt for rest.

On the previous day our eyes had been gladdened by the sight of a small well, where we filled our water-skins, therefore we were enabled to take our ease; although being in an entirely unfamiliar country, the watchfulness of our sentries was never for a single instant relinquished. We were travelling with the sun only as our guide, therefore knew not into what territory we had entered, save that it was as barren and inhospitable a region as it had ever been our lot to encounter,—a shadowless land of solitude, abandonment, and misery.

In our raid upon the caravan near Lake Tsâd a bundle of papers had come into our possession, and these had been handed to me; but travelling constantly, I had not had time or inclination to examine them. That night, however, alone in my tent, I untied them and spread them out. Most of them, including a kind of diary, were written in the language of the Roumis, and as some bore the image of the Liberty of the Franks, I concluded that they must have belonged to some French officer in the northern region of the Desert, who had probably perished in an attempt to penetrate south.

One paper, however, the last I took up, was written in my own tongue, and I read it eagerly. It was an official letter, dated from Paris, urging its recipient to secure, if possible, during his explorations, the *Fatassi* of Koti, as the French Government were extremely anxious to obtain possession of it, and by that letter offered to pay any sheikh or tribesman almost any sum in exchange for it.

I put the letter down, smiled, and resumed my pipe. The hapless explorer, whoever he was, had probably died, and certainly his hopes would never be realised, for the *Fatassi* of the learned Koti was the phantom book of the Soudan. There was not a clansman in the whole of the Great Desert who did not know all about that priceless volume, yet no one had ever seen it. It had been lost to the world for ages.

Mohaman Koti, or Koutou, the great marabout, lived in Timbuktu in the year 850 of the Hegira, and was the most esteemed and even tyrannical councillor of our ancestor, its powerful king. His authority is said to have originated in the following manner. The king one day distributed some dried dates to his court, and Koti, who had recently arrived, was overlooked. Shortly afterwards the learned councillor assembled a number of people and dispensed fresh dates among them. This miracle—for we have no dates in that region of the far south—having reached the king's ears, he discerned that upon Koti was set the divine seal, and from that moment gave him all his confidence. A few years later, according to Tarik è Sudan, Koti edited a history of the Kingdoms of Ganata, Songhoi, and Timbuktu, the only history written of those once all-powerful centres of civilisation, and in addition he dealt with the concerns of many peoples and many men. Families, since grown rich and powerful, and the chiefs of various countries, were shown to be with very humble origins, sometimes being the offspring of slaves. But while the book was being written, news was conveyed to the King of Timbuktu that the Songhois had revolted, and had combined with the great nation of Mossi to attack and capture his capital; therefore, in order to save his great store of treasure, he at once had it made up into single camel-loads, taken out of the city, and secreted in various distant spots on the confines of his empire. It was necessary, of course, to keep a strict and minute description of each spot where the wealth of the capital was concealed, in order that it might be recovered after the war; therefore Koti was ordered to inscribe in his book instructions how to unearth the great store of gold and gems, the spoils of war during four centuries. This, according to a legend completely borne out by our Tarik, he did, and the precious manuscript was given into the king's own keeping. Ere one moon, however, the learned historian died suddenly at Tindirma, where a little white mosquelike house marks his grave till this day. The war was fought, proving, alas! disastrous to the king, who was compelled to fly, but, strangely enough the Tarik maintains silence regarding his subsequent adventures, or of what became of the precious *Fatassi*. Legend has it that the king was treacherously poisoned by a slave, as rulers were apt to be in those turbulent days; but by whatever means the once-powerful monarch met with his death, the fact remains that the priceless volume and guide to the enormous treasure of ancient Timbuktu was lost to all. For more than four centuries the recovery of the *Fatassi* has been the dream of poor and rich alike. The scholar coveted it because it would shed so much light upon the obscure past of these vast regions; the camel-driver, the merchant, and the prince alike desired to possess it for the information it was known to contain regarding the long-lost wealth.

"'STAY,' SHE WHISPERED."

P. 212.

It was because of the latter that the government of the Franks desired to obtain it. But theirs, like my own, was but a vain desire.

A whole moon passed, and still we pressed forward towards Gao, ever in the crimson track of the setting sun. One night, however, when the camp was asleep, the guards raised the alarm, but so suddenly were we attacked that we scarce had time to defend ourselves from a column of French Spahis who had swept down upon us. It was a mad, terrible rush. Although our tribesmen fought valiantly and well, it was impossible to withstand the frightful hail of bullets poured forth upon us by a gun they carried which spat forth lead in deadly hail. Our men, seeing the havoc wrought by this new weapon, turned and fled. Fortunately the poison-wind had sprung up, and its clouds of sand cannot be faced by the men of the north; therefore we were enabled to escape, although unfortunately compelled to leave the greater part of the stolen camels and merchandise in their possession.

As, in the confusion, I sprang upon a horse and rode through the blinding sandstorm for my life, I heard the thud of the horses' hoofs of my pursuers. From the noise there must have been a score of men, anxious, no doubt, to secure the marauding chief feared by all the caravans. But swift as the wind itself, I rode on alone the greater part of that hot, stifling night, until, pulling up, dismounting, and placing my ear to the ground, I could, detect no sound of pursuit. In the glimmering twilight, as night gave place to day, I saw before me a huge, dark rock, shaped like a camel's hump, rising from the sand, and, riding onward, I there tethered my horse beneath it, and flung myself down to snatch an hour's sleep ere the sun rose, intending then to go forth again and rejoin my scattered people.

How long mine eyes were closed Allah alone knoweth; but when I opened them I found myself lying on a panther's skin in a darkened chamber, filled with the music of running water. The place was cooled by the stream, and in the dim recesses of the room I could distinguish rich divans. Suspended from the roof was a fine Moorish lamp of chased gold, which shed a soft, yellow light, and from a perfuming-pan was diffused the sweet odour of attar of rose. The light was soft and restful, and in wonder I rubbed my eyes and gazed about me.

"Allah give thee peace, O stranger!" a thin squeaking voice exclaimed. And glancing quickly behind me, I beheld a wizen-faced man, small of stature, dressed in a robe of bright blue silk, and so bent by age that his white beard almost swept the ground. Notwithstanding his venerable appearance, however, his face was dark and forbidding, and his small, black piercing eyes, that time had not dimmed, had a glint of evil in them. Instinctively, ere we had spoken a dozen words, I mistrusted him.

"To whose hospitality do I owe the rest and repose I have enjoyed?" I inquired, slowly rising to my feet and stretching my cramped limbs.

"My name," the old man croaked, "is Ibn Batouba. I discovered thee sleeping in the sun outside this my dwelling-place, and brought thee in, for the rays had smitten thee with a grievous sickness, and thou wert on the point of death. Thou hast remained here twelve days."

"Twelve days!" I cried, with incredulity, at the same moment feeling my head reeling. "Then to thee I owe my life?"

The hideous old man in blue grinned with satisfaction, regarding me with a strange, covert glance.

By this time my eyes had grown accustomed to the semi-darkness, and I saw that the chamber was a natural one—a kind of arched cavern, the floor of which had been levelled, and a channel formed for the cool spring that bubbled forth and rippled away into gloomy depths.

"This thy dwelling is beneath the surface of the earth," I observed, glancing around me. "Why dwellest thou here in secret?"

"The true Arab answereth not the question of Ahamadou, Sheikh of the Azjar Touaregs," he replied, with a sneering accentuation on the final word. "Allah hath sent thee as my guest; partake of all that I have, but seek no explanation of who or of what I am."

He evidently recognised me, and his strange words puzzled me. First, I had no idea that such a luxurious abode could exist in the centre of that inhospitable region; secondly, the very fact pointed to the conclusion that in my flight I had approached near to a town; but thirdly, I had already proof positive that my strange host, the man who declared he had saved my life, lied to me. At the well where we had halted on the day before the fight, I had plucked a sprig of jasmine, and placed a tiny piece behind my ear, beneath the black nicab around my head. This I recollected, and, taking it in my hand, found it still limp and undried. By that alone I knew I had not been there many hours, and that his story was untrue.

I suggested that I should be reluctantly compelled to leave; but he at once became profuse in his hospitality.

"No, not yet," he urged. "I am alone, save for my slaves, and thy companionship is pleasant. Remain, and I will show thee over this my hidden dwelling-place. It may interest thee." And taking down a torch, he lit it and led the way across a tiny bridge that spanned the running water, and opening a door in the rock, conducted me through several intricate passages, narrow and dark, until we came to a series of caverns of various sizes, each hung with rich silken hangings, and the floors covered by the most beautiful carpets from the East. Over each a great golden lamp of filigree shed a soft light, showing how rich and costly were the antique tables of inlaid pearl and silver, and how wide and soft were the divans. In each the thin blue smoke, curling upward from the golden perfuming-pan, gave forth an intoxicating fragrance, and in one I noticed lying discarded a pair of tiny green slippers, embroidered with seed-pearls, and a ginkra, one of those little two-stringed guitars fashioned from a tortoise-shell, both betraying the presence of a woman.

When we had passed through half a dozen similar chambers in the solid rock, the old man, croaking as he went, stopped suddenly at the further end of the last and most gorgeous of all his subterranean domain, and with a grim expression on his evil countenance, said—

"And this is the Bab-el-Hâwiyat—the dreaded Gate of Evil, whence none return." I started, and drew back. Throughout the Desert there has been for all ages a legend that somewhere there exists the entrance to the dreaded kingdom of darkness where Eblis reigneth. He opened wide the small door; but there was only darkness impenetrable, and an odour of damp earth. Holding his torch aloft, he crossed the threshold, and bade me peer in. Then I distinguished, a few spans from where he stood, a great yawning chasm opening to the very bowels of the earth.

"Hearken!" he cried in his squeaking, uncanny voice, at the same time returning into the room and snatching up from one of the coffee-stools a large metal dish, which an instant later he hurled into the dark abyss.

I listened to ascertain its depth. But no sound came back. I shuddered, for I knew it was unfathomable.

As he faced me in closing the door I detected in his keen eyes a strange exultant look, and was seized by a sudden desire to ascend once again to the light of day. True, I could have crushed the life out of him as easily as I could crush a spider in my fingers, while in my belt was my jambiyah that had a score of times tasted the life-blood of mine enemies, yet he had not harmed me, and to kill one's host is forbidden by Al-Korân. Therefore I stayed my hand.

As we retraced our steps he poured upon me nauseating adulations, declaring me to be the most valiant sheikh in the Great Desert, and using the most extravagant simile of which the Arabic tongue is capable, a fact which in itself filled me with increasing suspicion. Suddenly, however, as we reached the chamber where flowed the cooling spring, the truth was made plain. As he opened the door two officers of the French, in linen garments and white helmets, who had apparently been lying in wait, pounced upon me, uttering loud cries of triumph.

The old white-bearded recluse—may Allah burn his vitals—had betrayed me. He had held me, and sent word to the Franks to come and capture their prize—Ahamadou, the chieftain of the Azjar. But in an instant I, upon whose head a price was set, drew my blade and defended myself, slashing vigorously right and left, succeeding at last in escaping down the dark winding passage through which we had just passed. Forward I dashed through room after room, upsetting some of the tables in my mad rush, while behind me were the white-faced officers with drawn swords, determined to take me alive or dead. Well I knew how desperate they were, and in that instant believed myself lost. Yet, determined to sell my life dearly, it flashed across my mind that rather than suffer the ignominy of being taken in chains to Algiers, the infidel city, and there tried by the tribunal as others had been, I would cast myself into the fathomless pit.

I sprang towards the small, low door, but at first could not open it. In a few moments the crafty Ibn Batouba, with the Franks, gained the spot; but I had already unlocked the door and flung it open. Then, just as they put out their hands to seize me, I swung aside, lifted my knife, and struck my evil-faced betrayer full to the heart.

With a piercing shriek he fell forward over the door lintel, and his lifeless body rolled into the awful chasm, while at the same instant I gave a bound, and with a cry of defiance, leaped down into the darkness after him.

I felt myself rushing through air, the wind whistling in my ears as deep down I went like a stone in the impenetrable gloom. Those moments seemed hours, until of a sudden a blow on the back knocked me half-insensible, and I found myself a second later wallowing in a bed of thick, soft dust. Instantly it occurred to me that because this carpet of dust deadened the sound of things pitched into the chasm, the belief had naturally arisen that it was unfathomable. I rose, but sank up to the knees in the soft sand, which, stirred by my fall, half-choked me. Far above, looking distant like a star, I saw the light of a torch. My infidel pursuers were peering into the fearsome place in chagrin that I had evaded them. The air, however, was hot and foul, and I knew that to save my life I must be moving; therefore, with both hands outstretched,

I groped about, amazed to discover the great extent of this natural cleft in the earth, formed undoubtedly by some earthquake in a remote age.

Once I stumbled, and bending, felt at my feet the still warm body of my betrayer—may Eblis rend him. I drew my jambiyah from his breast, and replaced it in its sheath. Then, tearing from his body the silken gauze which formed his girdle, I fashioned a torch, igniting it after some difficulty with my steel. Around me was only an appalling darkness, and I feared to test the extent of the place by shouting, lest my pursuers above should hear. So forward I toiled in a straight line, floundering at every step in the dust of ages, until the cleft narrowed and became tunnel-like with a hard floor. I stooped to feel it, and was astounded to discover that the rock had been worn smooth and hollow by the tramp of many feet.

Besides, the air had become distinctly fresher, and this fact renewed courage within me. At first I felt myself doomed to die like a fox in a trap; but with hope reawakened there might, after all, I thought, be some outlet.

Of a sudden, however, there arose before me a colossal female figure seated on a kind of stool, with features so hideous and repulsive that I drew back with an involuntary cry. It was a score times as high as myself, and as I hold my torch above my head to examine it, I saw it was of some white, semi-transparent stone of a kind I had never before beheld. The robes were coloured scarlet and bright blue, and the face and hands were tinted to resemble life. One hand was outstretched. On the brow was a chaplet of wonderful pearls, and on the colossal fingers, each as thick as my own wrist, were massive golden rings which sparkled with gems. But the sinister grinning countenance was indeed that of a high-priestess of Eblis.

In amazement I held my breath and gazed about me. Around the sides of the cavern were ranged many other smaller female figures, seated like the central one, and the face of each bore a hideous, repulsive grin, as if in mockery of my misfortunes. Before the great central colossus was a small triangular stone altar, upon which was some object. I crossed, and glancing at it found to my dismay that it was a beautiful and very ancient illuminated manuscript of our holy Korân. But through it had been thrust a poignard, now red with rust, and it had been torn, slashed, and otherwise defiled.

The truth then dawned upon me that this noisome place into which I had plunged was actually the abode of the ancient and accursed sect who worshipped Eblis as their god.

As I gazed wonderingly about me, I saw everywhere evidence that for ages no foot of man had entered that dark silent chamber. The dust of centuries lay smooth and untrodden.

Again I passed beneath the ponderous feet of the gigantic statue, when suddenly my eyes were attracted by an inscription in Kufic, the ancient language of the marabouts, traced in geometrical design upon the hem of the idol's garment. My torch had burned dim, so I lit another, and by its flickering rays succeeded in deciphering the following words:—

"Lo! I am Azour, wife of Eblis, and Queen of all Things Beneath the Earth. To me, all bow, for I hold its riches in the hollow of my hand."

I glanced up quickly, and there, far above, I distinguished that in the idol's open palm there lay some object which the fickle flame of my torch could not reveal. But consumed by curiosity, I at once resolved to clamber up and ascertain what riches lay there. With extreme difficulty, and holding my flambeau in my left hand, I managed at length to reach the platform formed by the knees of the figure, and then scrambled up the breast and along the outstretched arm. But on mounting the latter, I was dismayed to discover that the object for which I had toiled was neither gold, silver, nor gems, but merely a brown and mouldy parchment scroll. Standing at last upon the open hand, I bent and picked it up; but in an instant I recognised that my find was of priceless value. Ere I had read three lines of the beautifully formed but sadly faded Arabic characters, I knew that it was none other than the long-sought manuscript of the *Fatassi*, the mysterious phantom book of the Soudan.

I placed my treasure beneath my dissa, and at once proceeded to descend, eager to discover some means of escape from that gloomy cavern, peopled by its hideous ghosts of a pagan past. In frantic haste I sought means of exit; but not until several hours had elapsed did I succeed in entering a burrow which, leading out into a barren ravine in the desert, had once, no doubt, been used as entrance to the secret temple of those who believed not in the One Merciful, but in Eblis and Azour.

After travelling many days, I succeeded in rejoining my people at a spot four marches from Gao, bearing concealed in my dissa the priceless history of my ancestors, with the minute plans for the recovery of their hidden treasure. At this moment the *Fatassi*, traced by the hand of Koti, so long coveted by the Franks, is in my possession; though only to two of my headmen have I imparted the secret that I have recovered it.

To seek to unearth the ancient treasure at present would be worse than useless, for our conquerors would at once despoil us. But when the great Jehad is at last fought, and more peaceful days dawn in the Soudan, then will the secret treasure-houses be opened and the Azjar become a power in the land, because of the inexhaustible riches left to them by their valiant ancestors for the re-establishment of their lost kingdom. Until then, they possess themselves in patience, and trust in the One.

To thee, O Reader of this my Tarik of toil and tumult, peace.

Chapter Nine.

The Father of the Hundred slaves.

Ahamadou, squatting upon his haunches before our camp fire, calmly smoking his long pipe, related to me the following story, declaring it to be a true incident. All wanderers in the Great Desert, be they Arabs or Touaregs, are born story-tellers, therefore I reproduce the narrative as he told it. It must be remembered that the Azjars were, at one period—not so very long ago—slavers who made many raids in the primeval forests south of Lake Tsâd, and that Ahamadou himself profited very considerably by that illegitimate trade. It was rumoured down at "the coast" that the leaders of these Touareg raiders were not Africans, and this story appears to substantiate a statement which was, at the time, ridiculed at the Colonial Office in London.

"Get up, you lazy devil. Stir yourself. We're in a complete hole!"

"Hole? hole? Ah, your English tongue is indeed extraordinary! A hole is a place in the ground, *n'est ce pas?*"

"Yes, and you'll have a hole in the ground all to yourself, my dear Pierre, if you don't bustle up a bit."

Pierre Dubois, the man addressed, a bronzed, grey-bearded, stout, small-eyed Belgian of fifty, was lying tranquilly on his back on a pile of soft rugs, like an Oriental potentate, smoking his *shisha*, or travelling pipe, and being fanned by an extremely ugly negress. Dubois was the name he had adopted after leaving the Congo hurriedly, carrying with him a goodly sum belonging to the Belgian Government, in whose employ he had been for ten years. A native of Liège, he was one of the pioneers of that so-called Central African civilisation of trade, gin, and the whip; but after lining his pockets well, and making good his escape through the boundless virgin forests of "darkest Africa," he had started as a trader in that most marketable of all commodities—black ivory.

Pierre Dubois and Henry Snape, his partner, were slave-raiders. They dressed as Arabs, and lived as Arabs.

Outside in the blazing noon, beneath the scanty shade of a few palms and mimosa scrub which surrounded that desert watering-place known as Akdul, a number of their heavily-armed followers were lying stretched upon the sand, sleeping soundly after their two-bow prayer to Allah, while here and there alone sat one of their number on his haunches, wrapped in his white burnouse, hugging his knees, his rifle at his side, keeping watch. They were a forbidding, evil-looking lot these Songhoi Touaregs, pirates of the forests and the desert, each with his black *litham* wrapped around his face concealing his features, a complete arsenal of weapons in his girdle, a string of charms sewn in little bags of yellow leather around his neck, and, strapped beneath his left arm, a short cross-kilted sword, keen-edged as a razor.

Beyond, lying in the full sun glare, were sixty or seventy wretched, woolly-haired negroes, men and women, chained together and guarded by a dozen of the veiled men. Throughout Northern and Central Africa the very name of the Songhoi was synonymous with all that was fierce, cruel, and relentless, for they lived by robbing the desert caravans or capturing slaves in the boundless virgin forests between the Niger and the Congo, being essentially a nomadic race, and having no other home than their tents in the Sahara, that limitless wilderness of rock and sand. Of all the slavers of Central Africa these "veiled men" were the worst, for they attacked and burned villages, placed the unfortunate blacks to torture to compel them to reveal the hiding-places of their store of ivory, and afterwards took them prisoners, and sold them in the great central slave-market at El Obeïd, away in Kordofan.

Among the natives of the Upper Congo and the Aruwimi, even the hordes of that notorious king of slavers, Tippu-Tib,—so called by the negroes because the guns of his men created a noise, from which they have named him phonetically,—were more tolerated than the fierce Songhoi bands, with their black veils, which none ever removed, sleeping or waking; for the track of the latter through the forest or grass-land was always marked by murder, devastation, and wanton cruelty.

Dubois, when in the service of King Leopold, had been active in endeavouring to put down the trade, but seeing how lucrative it was, and finding Snape, an English adventurer, ready to join him, he had collected a following of the fiercest Touaregs he could gather, and as he paid all well for their services, while on their part they were proud to be led by a white man in whom they had once lived in fear, their trade had, for a long time, been a most lucrative one. They were the terror of the whole region from Stanley Falls to Tanganyika. A dozen times they had been north to El Obeïd with ivory of both varieties, white and black, and on each occasion the profits had been far beyond their expectations. The trade is still easy enough in the Congo State, and slaves are captured without very much difficulty. The great risk, however, is to transport them by the route they had been following for the past two months, as, in order to reach the central market, they had to pass through that portion of British territory where a very watchful eye is kept, and where the notorious Arab raider Kilonga-Longa met his fate only a few months before.

But Dubois and Snape had run the gauntlet many times, and were absolutely fearless. On the present raid through the country of Emin and Junker, they had made their captures in the Moubouttou, within the Belgian sphere of influence, with the complicity of the Belgian agent at Sanga, whom they, of course, bribed with a goodly present of ivory; then, marching through the great Forest of Eternal Night, due northward to Zayadin, they had passed through the Dinka country to Fatik, which, being only two days' march from the Bahr-el-Guebel upon which the British have posts, is a dangerous point. Nevertheless, they had pushed forward night and day, and were now in the centre of that great, sunburnt desert, the Wilderness of Nouer, which stretches northward for three hundred miles to El Obeïd.

Dubois grumbled loudly at the Englishman for interrupting his meditations, saying—

"Go and sleep, *mon cher*. You'll be getting fever if you worry too much."

"Worry!" echoed Snape. "There's danger, I tell you. Surely you're not a confounded fool, man?"

"Ah," answered his partner, quite calmly, "is there not always danger here, in Africa? You have a wonderful imagination, my dear Henri, I quite admit; but do allow me to finish my sleep. Then let us talk of this extraordinary hole, whatever it may be."

"Idiot!" ejaculated the Englishman, hitching up his flowing white burnouse. He was a tall, good-looking fellow of forty, whose career, however, had been a singularly eventful one. Since he left Balliol he had met with a good many adventures in various lands, most of them being to his discredit. He had been a born gambler, and had drifted from the London clubs to the tables at Monte Carlo, and thence, by a very crooked channel, to that sink of the world, Africa, where chance had brought him in contact with the scoundrel and arch-slaver Dubois. They were a well-matched pair. At college Snape had taken honours for Arabic, therefore his knowledge of that language now served him in good stead. He was one of those men who could never run straight, even though he had often tried. He was a born outsider.

"Why idiot?" inquired his partner lazily. The old negress waved the fan backwards and forwards, understanding not a word of the conversation between the headman and the great white Sheikh, who, on account of his raiding, the Touaregs had named The Father of the Hundred Slaves.

"Well, I'm not the sort of fellow to let the grass grow under my feet when there's any danger," snapped Snape. "You remember what Zafar said yesterday."

"He's like yourself, *mon cher*,—always apprehensive of some horrible calamity," muttered the Belgian, blowing a cloud of smoke from his lips.

"This time, I tell you, it's no mere imagination," the Englishman went on. "Last night, after the *dua*, I left secretly, so as not to arouse any misgivings, and rode due east until the dawn, when I discovered, encamped among the *aghrad*, a whole troop of Soudanese soldiers. I got near enough to ascertain that the officers were Englishmen."

"Well?"

"They've got word somehow that we are passing through," he said. "And now, if you don't stir yourself, you'll never see Brussels again—you understand?"

"I have no wish to see Bruxelles, *mon cher*," the elder man replied, quite undisturbed. "If I did, it would only be to see the inside of a prison. No; I prefer Africa to the pleasures of the miniature Paris. Here, if one has a little ivory, one is a king. Life is very pleasant."

"I admit that," his companion said. "But do, for Heaven's sake, get up and let us decide what to do. There's danger, and we can't afford to be trapped, especially with all those niggers tied in a string. The evidence is a bit too strong against us, and the officers are English. There's no bribing *them*, you know."

The Belgian stirred himself lazily at last, and asked—

"Are they at a well?"

"No. They are without water."

"Then as this is the only well for about a hundred miles, they'll arrive here to-day—eh?"

"Of course. That's why I came straight to warn you. There's no time to be lost. Let's strike camp and get away. It's skip or fight."

"If we skeep—I suppose you mean march—ah! your English language!—then they will skeep in pretty quick time after us. They've got wind of our presence in the vicinity, therefore why not remain and fight?"

"Fight my own people?" cried Snape. "No, I'm damned if I do!"

"Why not?" asked the Belgian, with gesticulation. "Our Touaregs will slice them into mincemeat. Besides, at long range they're as good shots, and better, than those Soudanese, all fez and swagger."

"No," the Englishman argued. "Let's fly now, while there's time. In two days we shall be in the Nioukour, and they'll never find us in the mountains. We hid there quite snugly once before, you recollect."

"Muhala," said the Belgian, turning to the old negress, "go. Call Yakub, and remain outside."

The hideous old woman went forth into the sun glare, and in a few moments an old thin-faced Touareg entered, making a low salaam.

"Now, Yakub," exclaimed the Belgian in Arabic, "answer me. Of what did our caravan consist when we left the Aruwimi?"

"Three hundred and thirty-three slaves, and twenty-nine tusks," answered the villainous-looking old fellow.

"And now?"

"Seventy-three blacks and twenty-nine tusks."

"Then two hundred and sixty have died?"

"Yea, O master," he responded. "The new lash of elephant hide has killed many, and the black death has been responsible for the remainder. Five are suffering from it now, and never a day passes ere one or more is not attacked. I have feared that none will live to sight the mosques of El Obeïd."

"In short, Yakub, they are a diseased lot—eh? You think they're worthless?"

"Only two women are left, O master, and both were seized by the black death yesterday."

"In that case," observed the Belgian, turning to his partner, "the whole batch are not worth transporting. The game is not, as you English say, worth the lamp."

"Then what's your suggestion?" asked Snape.

"Well, as you are so much in fear of these confounded English, we must, I suppose, act."

"How?"

"It is quite simple. We just abandon the whole lot, and save ourselves and the ivory."

"Very well," his companion agreed. "I'm open to any move except fighting against the English."

"Bah! You are full of scruples, *mon cher* Henri," he laughed. "I have none—none. And I am happy—perfectly happy." He was silent a moment, as though reflecting deeply.

"But," he added, "I do wish we could teach these interfering English a lesson. It would do them good. They try to rule Africa nowadays. Ah! if we could—if we could!" And there was a strange glint of evil in his eyes.

An hour later Dubois and Snape, at the head of their formidable troop of brigandish horsemen, were riding at full speed across the desert due west, towards the far distant forest of Dyonkor, it having been decided to skirt this, and then travel south for a fresh raid in Congo territory.

As for the poor wretches bound together, and dying of thirst and disease, they were still secured to the palm trunks and abandoned to their fate, tortured by being within sight of the well, yet unable to slake the frightful thirst consuming them. Dwellers in the damp, gloomy forest, where the sunlight never penetrates, the intense heat of the desert struck them down one after another, sending them insane or killing them outright.

Time after time Snape turned in his high Arab saddle, glancing back apprehensively to see if they were followed. But his partner only laughed sarcastically, saying—"You still fear your friends the English? Ah! you have the heart of the chicken. All is quite unnecessary. We have made them a present of the whole lot, and I hope they will appreciate our kindness. Now we shall take it easy, and hope for better fortune with the next batch. I fancy that the new lash must be too hard. The women can't stand it, so it seems."

"A little less whipping and a little more water would keep 'em in better condition," Snape observed. "Yakub is eternally lashing them for some imaginary laziness or offence."

"Yes, it's all due to that new lash," the Belgian admitted. "It must be used with less frequency on the next lot."

"It's a revolting punishment. Twenty blows kill a strong nigger," his companion declared. "The thing ought to be thrown away."

"Ah, yes," sneered his companion. "You would, if you had your own way, keep women to brash the flies off them, and carry feather-beds for them to sleep on. You always forget that you are not dealing with civilised beings. They're mere niggers."

"Well, we're not of the most civilised type, you and I, if the unwelcome truth be told," the Englishman responded. "If we are trapped there'll be a howl in Europe."

"But I, for one, don't mean to be caught," laughed the Belgian gaily, with perfect confidence of his security. And they both rode side by side, the troop of white-burnoused Pirates of the Desert thundering on behind, raising a cloud of dust which, in that clear atmosphere, could be seen many miles away.

On, on they sped over the burning sand, riding easily at a hand gallop, without a halt, the black-veiled raiders laughing and chaffing, chattering, pushing forward, even in the blood-red track of the dying day.

Night fell quickly, as it does in that region. The slavers encamped in a sandy hollow beneath the rocks, and Dubois, ordering the tent to be pitched, sat smoking with his partner after the dish of *dakkwa* (pounded Guinea-corn with dates) which old Muhala had prepared. They were alone.

"To camp like this before we reach the forest is, to my mind, simply inviting capture," Snape grumbled. "The military detachment is evidently out in search of us, and the little lot we've abandoned will point out to them the direction we've taken. Then they'll follow and overtake us."

"Oh no, they won't," answered the Belgian, with a serene smile.

"What makes you so sure?"

"Remember that, coming up from the river, they must have been at least six days without water; therefore they'll halt at Akdul to drink and fill their water-skins before pushing forward."

"Well?" inquired Snape.

The crafty Belgian looked curiously into the face of his companion, and smiled grimly.

"Well, if they halt there," he said, "they won't trouble us any more."

"I don't understand."

"I doctored the water before we left. That's why I didn't leave the blacks loose to drink it."

"What!" gasped the Englishman wildly, starting to his feet. "You've actually poisoned the well?"

The Belgian nodded and laughed, without removing his *shisha* from his lips.

"You scoundrel! You fiend!" the Englishman shouted, his face white with passion. "I've done some shabby tricks in my time, but, by Heaven! I'd rather have given myself up than have assented to the wholesale murder of my own people like that!"

A sarcastic smile crossed the Belgian's sinister features.

"Excitement is entirely unnecessary, *mon cher* Henri," he said, calmly. "It may, you know, bring on a touch of fever. Besides, by this time there isn't many of them, white or black, left to tell the tale. Yakub, whom I left behind to watch, has just come in to report that they arrived an hour after we had left, released the slaves, and watered freely, enjoying themselves immensely. Before he started to return, fully fifty were dead or dying, including all the white officers. But why trouble further? We've saved ourselves."

"Trouble!" roared Snape, his eyes flashing with a fierce fire of indignation, "Get up, you infernal scoundrel, or I'll shoot you as you lie! You're an outlaw; so am I. Trouble! Why, one of those white officers was Jack Myddleton, my brother, and," he added in a harsh tone—"and I'm going to avenge his death!" Instantly Dubois saw his partner's intention, and sprang to his feet, revolver in hand.

Two reports sounded almost simultaneously, but only one man fell. It was the Belgian, who, with an imprecation on his lips, dropped back with a bullet through his temple, and in a few seconds expired.

At dawn Muhala discovered her master dead, and his companion missing. Search was at once made for the Englishman, who was found lying dead upon the sand half a mile from the camp.

He had committed suicide.

Around the well of Akdul the caravans that water there in crossing the arid wilderness still see quantities of bones of horses and of men. Long ago the vultures have stripped them, and they now lie bleaching in the sun, a mute record of a coward's treachery, of the revolting vengeance of The Father of the Hundred Slaves.

Chapter Ten.

The Mystery of Afo.

In the mystic haze of the slowly dying day, mounted on a *méheri*, or swift camel, I carried my long rifle high above my head, and rode speedily over the great silent wilderness of treacherous, ever-shifting sand. Once I drew rein to listen, turning my eyes to the left, where the distant serrated crests of the mountains of Nanagamma loomed forth like giant shadows; but as nothing broke the appalling stillness, I, a mere tribesman then, sped forward again, reaching a small oasis, where I made my camel kneel, and then dismounted.

As I strode towards the lonely shrine of Sidi Okbar—a small doomed building constructed of sun-dried mud, under which reposed the remains of one of our most venerated marabouts—I fear my burnouse was brown, ragged, and travel-stained; the haick that surrounded my face was torn and soiled, and upon my feet were rough, heavy slippers, sadly the worse for wear. The latter, however, I kicked off on approaching the shrine; then, kneeling close to the sun-blanched wall, cast sand upon myself, kissed the earth, and, drawing my palms down my face, repeated the Testification. In fervent supplication I bowed repeatedly, and, raising my voice until it sounded distinct on the still air, invoked the blessing of Allah.

"O Merciful! O beneficent Grantor of Requests!" I cried; "O King of the day of Faith, guide us, ere to-morrow's sun hath run its course, into the path that is straight, and leadeth unto the *kasbah* of our enemies of Abea. Strengthen our arms, lead us in times of darkness and in the hours of day, destroy our enemies, and let them writhe in Al-Hâwiyat, the place prepared for infidels, where their meat shall be venomous serpents, and they shall slake their thirst with boiling pitch."

Startled suddenly by a strange sound, I listened with bated breath. The thought occurred to me that my words might have been overheard by some spy, and instinctively my hand drew from my belt my *jambiyah*, the long, crooked dagger that I always carried. Again a noise like a deep-drawn sigh broke the silence, and I sprang to my feet and rushed round to the opposite side of the building, just in time to see a fluttering white robe disappearing in the gloom. Quick as lightning I sprang towards it, and in twenty paces had overtaken the eavesdropper, who, with a slight scream, fell to earth beneath my heavy hand.

"Rise!" I cried, roughly dragging the figure to its feet. "Thou son of Eblis!" Next second, however, I discovered that the fugitive was a woman, veiled, enshrouded in her haick, and wearing those baggy white trousers that render the Arab females hideous when out of doors.

"Thou hast overheard my orison," I cried, raising my knife. "Speak! speak! or of a verity will I strike!"

But the mysterious woman uttered no word, and in a frenzy of desperation I tore the veil from her face.

Aghast I stood; the knife fell from my lingers. The countenance revealed was amazingly beautiful, so charming, indeed, that instantly I became entranced by its loveliness, and stood speechless and abashed.

She was not more than eighteen, and her features were regular, with a fair complexion, a pair of brilliant dark eyes set well apart under browns blackened by kohl, and a forehead half-hidden by strings of golden sequins that tinkled musically each time she moved. Upon her head was set jauntily a little scarlet *chachia*, trimmed heavily with seed-pearls, while her neck was encircled by strings of roughly-cut jacinths and turquoises, and in the folds of her silken haick there clung the subtle perfumes of the harem.

Slowly she lifted her fine eyes, still wet with tears, to mine, and, with her breast rising and falling quickly, trembled before me, fearing my wrath.

"Loosen thy tongue's strings!" I cried at last, grasping her slim white wrist with my rough, hard hand. "Thou art from Afo, the City in the Sky, and thou hast gained knowledge of our intended attack?"

"Thy lips, O stranger, speak the truth," she faltered.

"Why art thou here, and alone, so far from thine home on the crest of yonder peak?" I inquired, gazing at her in wonderment.

"I came hither for the same purpose as thyself," she answered seriously, looking straight into my face,—"to crave Allah's blessing."

"Art thou a dweller in the house of grief?" I asked. "Tell me why thou didst venture here alone."

She hesitated, toying nervously with the jewelled perfume-bottle suspended at her breast; then she answered, "I—I am betrothed to a man I hate. The Merciful Giver of Blessings alone can rescue me from a fate that is worse than death—a marriage without love."

"And who is forcing thee into this hateful union? If it is thy father, tell me his name?"

"Yes, it is my father. His name is Abd el Jelíl ben Séf e' Nasr, Sultan of Abea."

"The Sultan!" I cried in amazement. "Then thou art Kheira!" I added, for the extraordinary beauty of the only daughter of the Sultan of Abea was proverbial throughout the Great Desert, from Lake Tsâd, even to the Atlas.

"Yes," she replied. "And from thy speech and dress I know thou art of the Azjar, our deadliest enemies."

"True," I answered. "To-morrow my tribe, to the number of ten thousand, now lying concealed in the valley called Deforou, will swarm upon thine impregnable city and—"

"Ten thousand?" she gasped, pale and agitated. "And thou wilt kill my father, and reduce our people to slavery. Ah, no!" she added imploringly. "Save us, O stranger! Our fighting men went south one moon ago to collect the taxes at Dehagada, therefore we are unprotected. What can I do—how can I act to save my father?"

"Dost thou desire to save him, even though he would force upon thee this odious marriage?"

"I do," she cried. "I—I will save the City in the Sky at the cost of mine own life."

"To whom art thou betrothed," I asked, tenderly taking her hand.

"To the Agha Hassan è Rawi, who dwelleth at Zongra, beyond the Nanagamma. He is threescore years and ten, and 'tis said he treateth his wives with inhuman cruelty. One of his slaves told me so."

I stood silent and thoughtful. Though I was a member of a tribe who existed wholly upon loot obtained from the caravans and towns we attacked, yet so earnestly did the Sultan's daughter appeal, that all thought of preserving the secret of our intended attack by murdering her disappeared, and I found myself deeply in love. Mine was a poor chance, however, I told myself. The proud Sultan of Abea would never consent to a brigand as a son-in-law, even if she looked upon me with favour.

"To-night, O Daughter of the Sun, we meet as friends; to-morrow as enemies," I said. "Our spies have reported that thy city remaineth undefended, and, alas! there is a blood-feud between my people and thine; therefore, when the hosts of the Azjar enter with fire and sword, few, I fear, will be spared. Wilt thou not remain here with my tribesmen, and escape?"

"No," she answered proudly. "I am a woman of Afo, and I will return unto my people, even though I fall before to-morrow's sundown under thy merciless swords."

As she spoke, one hand rested upon her supple hip, and with the other she pointed to the high, shadowy peak whereon stood the great white stronghold known to the Kanouri people as The City in the Sky.

"But thou, who art like a sun among the stars, knowest our plans, and it is my duty to kill thee," I said, hitching my burnouse about my shoulders.

"I am in thine hands. If thou stainest them with my blood, thou wilt ever have upon thy conscience the remembrance that thou hast taken the life of one who was innocent of intrigue. If thou givest me freedom, I shall have at least one brief hour of felicity with my people before—before—"

And she sighed, without concluding the sentence.

"Thou, a fresh rose from the fountain-head of life, art in fear of a double fate,—the downfall of to-morrow, and the marriage feast next moon. Let not thy mind be troubled, for I stretch not forth the tongue to blame," I said at last, endeavouring to smile. "In Ahamadou, of the tribe Azjar, thou hast a devoted friend, and one who may peradventure assist thee in a manner thou hast not dreamed. Therefore mount thine horse and return with all speed to Afo—not, however, before thou hast given me some little souvenir of this strange meeting."

"Thou slakest my thirst with the beverage of kindness!" she cried in joy. "I knew when first I saw thee that thou wert my friend."

"Friend?—nay, lover," I answered gallantly, as, taking her tiny hand again, I pressed her henna-stained nails softly to my lips. She blushed and tried to draw away, but I held her firmly until she withdrew one of her gold bangles from her wrist, and, with a smile, placed it upon mine.

"Behold!" she exclaimed with a merry, rippling laugh, "it is thy badge of servitude to me!"

"I am a slave of the most handsome mistress in the world," I said happily. Then, urging her to warn the Sultan of the intentions of the Azjar, I kissed her once tenderly upon the lips, lifted her into the saddle of her gaily caparisoned horse, and then she twisted her torn veil about her face, and, giving me "Peace," sped away swift as an arrow into the darkness, bearing intelligence that would cause the utmost sensation in the mountain fastness.

"I love her," I murmured, when the sound of her horse's hoofs had died away. "But how can I save her? To-morrow, when we enter Afo and loot the Palace, she will be secured as slave. No!" I cried, "she shall never fall into Nikále's brutal hands—never while I have breath!"

The sound of whispering caused me to fix my gaze upon a dark shadow thrown by some ethel-bushes, and next second, half a dozen of my fellow tribesmen advanced.

"So, dog of a spy! thou hast betrayed us!" cried a voice, which in a moment I was startled to recognise as that of my enemy Mohammed El Sfaski.

"Yes," the others shouted with one accord; "we watched the son of offal speaking with the woman, and we overheard him telling her to warn the Sultan!"

"Follow her on the wings of haste!" cried El Sfaski. "Kill her, for death alone will place the seal of muteness upon the lips of such a jade." And in a few seconds two black-veiled figures vaulted into their saddles and tore past in the direction Kheira had disappeared.

"Speak!" thundered El Sfaski, who, with the others, had now surrounded me. "Knowest thou the punishment of traitors?"

"Yes," I answered, hoarsely.

"Who is the woman whose blackness and deceit hath captivated thee?"

Three rapid shots sounded in the distance. The men had evidently overtaken and murdered the daughter of the Sultan!

I held my breath.

"I—I refuse to give thee answer," I said, resolutely.

"By Allah! thou art a traitor to our lord and to our tribe, and of a verity thou hast also the eye of perfection. Therefore shalt thou die!" Then, turning to the others, he added—

"We have no time to bandy words with this accursed son of the Evil One. Tie him to yon tree, and let the vultures feast upon their carrion."

With loud imprecations the men seized me, tore off my haick and burnouse, and bound me securely to a palm trunk in such a position that I could only see the great expanse of barren sand. Then, with that refinement of cruelty of which the nomadic Azjar are past-masters, they smeared my face, hands, and feet with date-juice, to attract the ants and other insects; and, after jeering at me and condemning me to everlasting perdition and sempiternal culpability, they remounted their horses, and, laughing heartily, left me alone to wait the end.

Through the long, silent night, with arms and legs bound so tightly that I could not move them, I remained, wondering what terrible fate had befallen the beautiful girl who had overheard my orison. My two clansmen had not returned. I knew the men were splendid riders, therefore it was more than probable that they had very quickly overtaken her. Utterly hopeless, well knowing that to the blazing sun and the agonies of being half-devoured by insects I must very soon succumb, I waited, my ears on the alert to catch every sound.

In the sky a saffron streak showed on the edge of the sandy plain, heralding the sun's coming. I watched it gradually spread, knowing that each moment brought me nearer to an end of agony. I lifted my voice in supplication to Allah, and showered voluble curses upon the expedition about to be attempted by my tribe. The pale, handsome face of Kheira was ever before me, haunting me like a half-remembered dream, its beauty fascinating me, and even causing me to forget the horror of those hours of dawn.

Saffron changed to rose, and rose to gold, until the sun shone out, lighting up the trackless waste. The flies, awakened, began to torment me, and I knew that the merciless rays beating down upon my uncovered head would quickly produce the dreaded delirium of madness. The furnace heat of sunshine grew intense as noon approached, and I was compelled to keep my eyes closed to avoid the blinding glare.

Suddenly a noise fell upon my ear. At first it sounded like a low, distant rumbling; but soon my practised ears detected that it was the rattle of musketry and the din of tom-toms.

The City in the Sky was being attacked! My tribesmen had arranged to deliver the assault at noon, but what puzzled me was a sullen booming at frequent intervals. It was the sound of cannon, and showed plainly that Afo was being defended!

From where I was I could see nothing of it. Indeed, the base of the mountain was eight miles distant, and the city, perched upon its summit, could only be approached from the opposite side by a path that was almost inaccessible. Yet hour after hour the rapid firing continued, and it was evident a most desperate battle was being fought. This puzzled me, for had not Kheira said that the city was totally undefended? Still, the tumult of battle served to prevent me from lapsing into unconsciousness; and not until the sun sank in a brilliant, blood-red blaze did the firing cease. Then all grew silent again. The hot poison-wind from the desert caused the feathery heads of the palms to wave like funeral plumes, and night crept on. The horrible torture of the insects, the action of the sun upon my brain, the hunger, the thirst, and the constant strain of the nerves, proved too much; and I slept, haunted by spectral horrors, and a constant dread of the inevitable— that half-consciousness precursory of death.

So passed the second night, until the sun reappeared; but mine eyes opened not. The heat of the blazing noon caused me no concern, neither did the two great grey vultures that were hovering over me; for it was not until I heard voices in the vicinity that I gazed around.

One voice, louder than the others, was uttering thanks to Allah. I listened; then, summoning all my strength that remained, I cried aloud, in the name of the One Merciful, for assistance.

There were sounds of hurrying footsteps, voices raised in surprise, a woman's scream, and then objects, grotesquely distorted, whirled around me, and I knew no more.

When I again opened my weary, fevered eyes, I was amazed to find myself lying upon a soft, silken divan in a magnificent apartment, with slaves watching, ready to minister to my wants. I took a cooling draught from a crystal goblet handed to me, then raised myself, and inquired where I was. The slaves made no reply, but, bowing low, left. Then in a few moments the *frou-frou* of silk startled me, and next second I leaped to my feet, and, with a cry of joy, clasped Kheira in my arms.

In her gorgeous harem dress of pale rose silk, with golden bejewelled girdle, she looked bewitching, though around her eyes were dark rings that betrayed the anxiety of the past few days. As our lips met in hot, passionate kisses, she was followed by a tall, stately, dark-bearded man of matchless bearing, whose robe was of amaranth silk, and who wore in his head-dress a magnificent diamond aigrette. Kheira saw him, and withdrawing herself from my embrace, introduced me to her father, the Sultan of Abea.

"To thee I owe my life and my kingdom," said the potentate, giving me "Peace," and wringing my hand warmly. "Kheira hath related unto me the mercy thou didst show towards her; and it was thy word of warning that enabled us to repel and defeat the Azjar."

"Then thou, didst escape, O signet of the sphere of elegance!" I cried, turning to the Sultan's daughter.

"Yes; though I was hard pressed by two of thine horsemen, I took the secret path, and thus were they baffled."

"The Director of Fate apprised our fighting men of our danger," said the Sultan; "and they returned on the same night. The breeze of grace blew; the sun of the favour of Allah shone. The news brought by Kheira was quickly acted upon, and the defences of the city so strengthened, that when at noon the assault was delivered, our cannon swept thy tribesmen from the pass like grains of sand before the sirocco. For six hours they fought; but their attempts to storm the city gate were futile, and the handful of survivors were compelled to retire, leaving nearly five hundred prisoners, including your Sheikh himself, in our hands."

"And how was I rescued?" I inquired, after briefly explaining how my conversation with Kheira had been overheard.

"On the day following the fight, we went unto the shrine of Sidi Okbar to render thanks to Allah, and there found thee dying of heat and thirst. Thou didst sacrifice thy life to save our ruler and his city, therefore we brought thee hither," she said.

Then, taking my hands, the Sultan added, "Thou hast the verdure of the meadows of life. May Allah preserve thee, and grant unto thee long years of perfect peace, and an eternal rose-garden of happiness. Wipe off the rust of *ennui* and fatigue from the speculum of thy mind, and follow me; for a feast is already prepared for the celebration of this victory."

And we passed onward through the private pavilions—bewildering in their magnificence of marble and gold, and green with many leaves—to the Great Hall of the Divan, where, standing under the royal baldachin of yellow silk brocade, the Sultan of Abea rejoiced me with his favours, proclaiming me, Ahamadou, tribes man of the Azjar, the Saviour of the City in the Sky.

No Touareg has ever contracted marriage with an Arab; therefore, after tarrying in Afo for many moons, I made peace with my people and returned unto them, for the wild life of the limitless sands was more congenial to me than the ease and perfumes of palaces and the favours of kings.

Chapter Eleven.

The Throne of the Great Torture.

Far south, beyond the Atlas Mountains, beyond that great, limitless plain of the Talidat where nothing meets the aching eye but a dreary waste of red-brown, drifting sand, one experiences some curious phases of a life comparatively unknown, and little understood in European civilisation. There, life to-day is the same as it was ten centuries ago— the same as it will ever be: free and charming in its simplicity, yet with many terrors ever present, and sun-bleached bones ever reminding the lonely traveller that a pricked water-skin means the end of all things.

"LEFT ME ALONE TO WAIT THE END."

The Veiled Man — by William Le Queux

On a journey alone from Biskra to Mourzouk, in Fezzan, I foolishly disregarded the injunctions of my fellow tribesmen, and was rendered extremely uncomfortable by the astounding discovery that the camel caravan I had joined in Zaouia Timassanin, and with which I had been travelling for twenty days, belonged to the Kel-Izhaban, a tribe of marauders and outlaws with whom we had had for years a fierce blood-feud, and whose depredations and relentless butchery of their weaker neighbours caused them to be held in awe from Morocco across to Tripoli, and from Biskra to Lake Tsâd. In addition, I ascertained that the Sheikh, known to me as Sidi El-Adil, or "The Just," was really none other than Abdul-Melik, like myself, a pirate of the desert, against whom the French Government had sent three expeditions, and upon whose head a price had been set.

With bronzed, aquiline features, long grey beard, and keen, deep-set eyes; tall, erect, agile, and of commanding presence, he was a splendid specimen of the true-bred Arab of the plains. Though he expressed intense hatred for the Infidel, and invoked curses most terrible upon the horsemen of the Roumis in general, and those of the Azjar in particular, he, nevertheless, treated me with haughty courtesy, and extended to me the hand of friendship. As, at the head of our cavalcade of two hundred armed horsemen and a long string of camels, he rode day by day across the parched wilderness, interspersed by small sand-hills and naked ledges of rock, speckled with ethel-bushes half overwhelmed by sand, he was truly an imposing figure. His burnouse was of finest white wool, embroidered heavily with silk; the haick surrounding his face was of spotless china-silk, and around his head was wound many yards of brown camel's hair. The saddle upon which he sat was of crimson velvet, embroidered with gold and set with precious stones, and stirrups and spurs of massive silver completed the trappings of his splendid coal-black horse, which he managed with rare perfection and skill. On my white Ku-hai-lan stallion, I usually rode at his side, chatting to him in his own tongue, while two hundred of his people, erect in their saddles, and with their long-barrelled rifles slung behind, were ready to instantly execute his slightest wish.

The days were breathless and blazing. Scorched by the sun, and half-suffocated by the sand-laden wind, our way lay through a wilderness that Nature had forsaken. At night, however, when the outlaws of the desert had cast sand upon their feet and prayed their *maghrib*, and we had encamped under the palms of the oasis, eaten our dates and kouss-kouss, and slaked our thirst from our water-skins, then commenced the real luxury of the day—the luxury of idleness—as, reclining on a mat in front of the Sheikh's tent, with coffee and a cigarette, the great Abdul-

Melik would relate with slow distinctness stories of past encounters between his people and the hated Christians.

While sentries with loaded rifles kept a vigilant look-out lest we should be surprised by the ever-watchful Spahis or Chasseurs, half—a—dozen Arabs would squat in a semicircle before the great Sheikh, and, twanging upon their queer little banjos fashioned from tortoise-shells over which skin is stretched, would chant weirdly, in a strange staccato, Arab songs of love and war. At that hour a coolness falls over everything, intense silence reigns, the sky above grows a deeper and deeper blue, and the palms and talha trees look mysterious in the half-light. Soon the stars shine out like diamond points, and it grows darker and darker, until the chill night-breeze of the desert stirs the feathery heads of the date-palms. Then the lawless nomads, my companions, would wrap their burnouses closely about them, scoop out a hole in the warm sand, and there repose until the first flush of dawn.

About five weeks after I had inadvertently thrown in my lot with the Kel-Izhaban, and after penetrating a region that, as far as I am aware, has never been explored by Europeans—for it remains a blank upon the most recent map issued by the French Dépôt de la Guerre—we were one evening, at a spot evidently pre-arranged, joined by a body of three hundred horsemen, who armed themselves with the rifles they obtained from our camel's packs, and then, leaving the camels in charge of half-a-dozen men in a rocky valley called the Anzoua, we all continued our way in high spirits, jesting, laughing, and singing snatches of songs. Throughout that night, and during the following day, we rode at the same steady pace, with only brief halts that were absolutely necessary. On the second night darkness fell swiftly, but the moon rose, and under its bright mystic light we sped forward, until suddenly the gaunt man, in a dirty, ragged burnouse, who acted as our guide, shouted, and we pulled up quickly. Then, in the moonlight, I could just distinguish among the trees of the little oasis a few low, white houses, of what I subsequently learned was the little desert village of Tilouat, inhabited by the Kel-Emoghri, and distant ten leagues from the town of Idelès.

Abdul-Melik shouted an order, clear and distinct, whereupon the horsemen spread themselves out in two long lines, and with their guns carried across their saddles, the first line crept slowly and silently forward. By this movement I knew that we were about to attack the village, and held my own rifle ready for purposes of self-defence. Sitting in the second line, I advanced with the others, and the breathless moments that followed were full of excitement.

Suddenly a shot startled us, and at the same moment a muttered curse fell from the Sheikh's lips as he saw that our presence had been detected, for the shot had been fired in the village as a sound of warning. Almost instantly it was apparent that we had been betrayed, for a great body of horsemen galloped out to meet us, and in a few moments I found myself lying behind my horse pouring forth volley after volley from my rifle.

The fusillade was deafening, and for fully half an hour it was kept up. About twenty of our men had been killed or wounded, when suddenly the first line rose with loud shouts as if they were one man, and, mounting, rode straight at their opponents, while we followed at headlong speed upon our enemies almost ere they had time to realise our intention. The mêlée was awful. Swords, rifles, and keen, crooked *jambiyahs* were used with terrible effect, but very soon all resistance was at an end, and the work of looting the village commenced.

Half demented by excitement and success, my companions entered the houses, shot down the women with relentless cruelty, tore from them what little jewellery they possessed, and plundered, wrecked, and burned their homes out of sheer delight in destruction. I stood watching the terrible scene, but unable to avert the great calamity that had fallen so swiftly upon the peaceful little place. The fiendishness of our enemies had, alas! not been exaggerated. Abdul-Melik laughed gleefully, uttering some words as he rode past me swift as the wind. But I heeded him not; I loathed, despised, and hated him.

While dawn spread in rosy streaks, the work of plunder still proceeded, but when the sun shone forth, only the smoke-blackened walls of Tilouat remained standing. The plunder was quickly packed upon our horses, and soon afterwards we rode off, carrying with us twenty men and women who had been captured, all of whom would eventually find their way into the great slave-market, far away at Mourzouk.

At sundown, five days afterwards, we descended into a rocky valley, and suddenly came upon a wonderful mass of scattered ruins, of amazing magnitude and extent, which Abdul-Melik told me were the remains of a forgotten city called Tihodayen, and as we approached, I saw by the massive walls of hewn stone, the fallen columns half embedded in the sand, and by an inscription over an arched door, that they were relics of the Roman occupation. When we dismounted, I found that the ruined city gave shelter to the outlaws, and was their habitual hiding-place.

An hour later, reclining on mats under the wall of what had once been a great palace, the outlaw Sheikh and myself ate our evening meal of *saubusaj, beryseh,* and *luzinyeh,* and drank copiously of *dushab,* that luscious date-syrup which is so acceptable after the heat and burden of the Saharan day, while my companions feasted and made merry, for it appeared that they kept stores of food concealed there.

On commencing to smoke, Abdul-Melik ordered that the captives should be brought before him, and when, a few minutes later, they were ushered into his presence, they, with one exception, fell upon their knees, grovelled, and cried aloud for mercy. The single captive who begged no favour was a young, dark-haired girl of exquisite beauty, with black, piercing eyes, pretty, dimpled cheeks, and a complexion of almost European fairness. She wore a zouave of crimson velvet heavily embroidered with gold, a heavy golden girdle confined her waist, and her wide trousers were of palest rose-pink silk, while her tiny feet were thrust into velvet slippers of green embroidered with gold thread. But her dress had been torn in the fierce struggle with her pitiless captors, and as she stood, erect and defiant, with her hands secured behind her with a leathern thong, she cast at us a glance full of withering scorn.

The Sheikh raised his hand to command silence, but as her fellow-captives continued wailing, he ordered the removal of all but this girl, who apparently set him at defiance. Turning his keen eyes upon her, he noted how extremely handsome she was, and while she returned his gaze unflinchingly, her beauty held me in fascination. In all my journeys in the Land of the Sun I had never before seen such an absolutely perfect face.

"Who art thou?" demanded the dreaded chief, roughly. "What is thy name?"

"I am called Khadidja Fathma, daughter of Ali Ben Ushshâmi, cadi of Idelès," she answered, in a firm, defiant tone.

"Ali Ben Ushshâmi!" echoed Abdul-Melik, knitting his brows fiercely. "Thou art his daughter; the daughter of the accursed son of offal who endeavoured to betray me into the hands of the Roumis," he cried, exultantly. "I have kindled the lights of knowledge at the flambeau of prophecy, and I vowed that I would ere many moons seek vengeance."

"I have anticipated this thy wrath ever since thine horde of cowardly ruffians laid hands upon me," she answered, with a contemptuous toss of her pretty head. "But the daughter of the cadi of Idelès craveth not mercy from a servant of Eblis."

"Darest thou insult me, wench?" he cried, pale with passion, and starting up as if to strike her. "Thou art the child of the man who would have given me into the hands of the Spahis for the sake of the two bags of gold offered for my head. I will return his good offices by sending him to-morrow a present he will perhaps appreciate, the present of thine own hands. He will then be convinced that Abdul-Melik knoweth how to repay those who seek to injure him."

"Dost thou intend to strike off my hands?" she gasped, pale as death, nevertheless making a strenuous effort to remain calm.

"At sunrise the vultures will feast upon thee, and thine hands will be on their way to Idelès," he answered, with a sinister smile playing about his hard mouth.

"Malec hath already set his curse upon thee," she said, "and by each murder thou committest so thou createst for thyself a fresh torture in Al-Hâwiyat, where thy food will be offal and thou wilt slake thy thirst with boiling pitch. True, I have fallen captive into thine hands, having journeyed to Tilouat to see my father's mother who was dying; but thinkest thou that I fear thee? No!" she added with flashing eyes. "Though the people dread thee as the great and powerful Chief, I despise thee and all thy miserable parasites. If thou smitest off mine hands, it is but the same punishment as thou hast meted out to others of my sex. Thou art, after all, a mere coward who maketh war upon women."

"Silence, jade!" he cried, in a tumult of passion, and, turning to the men beside him, commanded: "Take her away, secure her alone till dawn, and then let her hands be struck off and brought to me."

Roughly the men dragged her away, but ere she went she cast at us a look of haughty scornfulness, and, shrugging her shoulders, treated this terrible mandate with ineffable disdain.

"The jade's hands shall be sent to her father, the Cadi, as a souvenir of the interest he taketh in my welfare," the Sheikh muttered aloud. "Her tongue will never again utter rebuke or insult. Verily, Allah hath delivered her into my hands a weapon to use against mine enemies."

I uttered eager words of intercession, pointing out the cruelty of taking her young life, but he only laughed derisively, and I was compelled to sit beside him while the other captives were questioned and inspected.

That night I sought repose in a shed that had been erected in a portion of the ruins, but found sleep impossible. The defiantly beautiful face of the young girl who was to die at dawn kept recurring to me with tantalising vividness, and at length I rose, determined if possible to save her. Noiselessly I crept out, my footsteps muffled by the sand, saddled one of Abdul-Melik's own horses, and without attracting the notice of either sentry on duty at each end of the encampment, I entered the ruin where, confined to an iron ring in the masonry by a leathern band, she crouched silent and thoughtful.

"*Fi amâni-illah!*" I whispered, as I approached. "I come to have speech with thee, and assist thee to escape."

"Art thou a friend?" she inquired, struggling to her feet and peering at me in the gloom.

"Yes, one who is determined that the outlaw's command shall never be executed," and taking the *jambiyah* from my girdle, I severed the thongs that confined her hands and ankles, and next second she was free.

Briefly I explained how I had saddled a fleet horse and placed a saddle-bag with food upon it.

"If I get safely away I shall owe my life to you," she said, with intense gratitude, pressing my hand for an instant to her quivering lips. "I know this place, and ere two moons can have risen I can travel through the rocky defile and be at my father's house in Idelès. Tell me thy name, so that my father may know who was his daughter's liberator."

I told her, and in the same hasty breath asked for some souvenir.

"Alas! I have nothing," she answered; "nothing but a strange ornament which my father's mother gave to me immediately before she died, an hour previous to the attack being made upon the village," and placing her hand deep into the breast of her dress she drew forth a rough disc of copper, about the size of a crown piece, with a hole in it, as if it had been strung upon a thread.

"When she gave it to me she told me it had been in her possession for years, that it was a talisman against terror, and that some curious legend was attached to it, the nature of which I do not now recollect. There is strange writing upon it in some foreign tongue of the Roumis that no one has been able to decipher."

I looked, but unable to detect anything in the darkness, I assured her that its possession would always remind me of her, and slipped it into the pocket of my gandoura.

"THE SINGLE CAPTIVE WHO BEGGED NO FAVOUR."
P. 291.

Then together we crept along under the shadow of the wall, and, gaining the spot where the horse stood in readiness, I held her for a second while she kissed my hand, uttering a fervent word of thanks, and afterwards assisted her into the saddle. Then a moment later, with a whispered "*Allah iselemeck!*" she sped away, with her unbound hair flying behind her, and was instantly lost in the darkness.

On realising that she had gone I was seized with regret, but feeling that at least I had saved her from a horrible doom, I returned to my little shed and, wrapping myself in my burnouse, slept soundly until the sun had risen high in the heavens.

Opening my eyes, I at once remembered Khadidja's quaint souvenir, and on examining it, was astonished to find both obverse and reverse of the roughly fashioned disc covered with an inscription in English crudely engraved, or rather scratched, apparently with the point of a knife. Investigating it closely I was enabled, after some difficulty, for I have only an elementary knowledge of the tongue of the Roumis, to read the following surprising words:—

"This record I leave for the person into whose hands it may fall, for I am starving. Whosoever reads this let him hasten to Zemnou, in the Zelaf Desert, two days from the well of El Ameïma, and from the Bab-el-Oued pace twenty steps westward outside the city wall, and under the second bastion let him dig. There will he be rewarded. John Edward Chatteris, held captive in the Kasbah of Borku by order of the Sultan 'Othmân, Sunday, June 13, 1843."

Chatteris! Instantly it occurred to me that a celebrated English explorer, archaeologist, and member of the Royal Geographical Society of that name, had years ago been lost, and his fate had remained a complete mystery. Inquiries for news of him had been circulated throughout the great Desert among the wandering tribes, with an offer of a reward. This, then, was a message inscribed, with apparent difficulty within the impregnable citadel of the warrior Sultan of Borku, whose little mountain kingdom was situate five hundred miles south of Mourzouk, between the Tibesti Mountains and Lake Tsâd; a secret that for half a century had been in the keeping of those who could not decipher it.

What might not be buried at the spot indicated by this curious relic of the great traveller? My curiosity was excited to the utmost. Impatient to investigate the truth, but compelled, nevertheless, to remain patient until such time as I could escape from my undesirable companions, I concealed the disc and rose to join Abdul-Melik at his morning meal.

Khadidja's escape caused the old outlaw intense chagrin, and his anger knew no bounds, but luckily no suspicion fell upon me, and having remained with them during two whole moons I succeeded one day, when we were near the town of Rhat, in evading them and getting away. As quickly as possible I returned to In Salah, where I exhibited the metal disc with its strange inscription to our three headmen, who became at once interested in it, announcing their intention to accompany me next day to investigate the truth of the engraved record.

With an escort of twenty of our men, all well mounted and armed, we rode out of In Salah at dawn, and for nine days continued our journey across the desert due eastward, first taking the caravan route to Tarz Oulli, beyond the French boundary, and continuing through the rocky region of the Ihéhaonen and across the Djedid Oasis, until one evening, at the *maghrib* hour, the high white walls and three tall minarets of the desert city of Zemnou came within view. It was unsafe to take our men nearer, therefore we returned and bivouacked until darkness set in. Then, dressed in the haick and burnouse of the Arab of the plain, the three headmen with myself, carrying spades concealed beneath our flowing drapery, approached the town and crept under the shadow of the walls, until we reached the Bab-el-Oued, or principal gate. Guarded by strong watch-towers on either side, the gate was closed, and silently we crept, anxious and breathless, on over the sand westward until we had counted twenty paces and reached the second bastion.

Then, after glancing eagerly around to reassure ourselves that we were not observed, we all five commenced to dig beneath the wall. Discovery, we knew, would mean death. The sand was loose, but full of stones, and for some time we worked without result. Indeed, I began to fear that someone had already been able to decipher the record and obeyed its injunctions, when suddenly the spade of one of my companions struck something hard, and he uttered an ejaculation. With one accord we worked with a will, and within ten minutes were unearthing an object of extraordinary shape.

At first it puzzled us considerably, but at length, when we had cleared the earth sufficiently to remove it, we made a cursory examination by the aid of wax tapers, and discovered that it was a kind of stool with a semi-circular seat, supported by six short columns of twisted gold in imitation of serpents, the seat itself being of gold inlaid with many precious stones, while the feet consisted of six great yellow topazes, beautifully cut and highly polished, held in the serpents' mouths. The gold had become dimmed by long contact with the earth, but the gems, as we rubbed off the dirt that clung to them, gleamed and sparkled in the tapers' fitful rays.

The stool, or throne, was so heavy that it was with difficulty two men dragged it out of the trench, and breathless with anxiety we all lent a willing hand to carry it over the five miles of open desert to where the men were awaiting us. Our arrival was greeted with cheers, but quickly the strange relic was wrapped in saddlebags and secured upon the back of a spare horse. At once we set out on the first stage of our return journey, reaching In Salah in safety ten days later, and learning with satisfaction on our arrival that Abdul-Melik had, during our absence, been killed in a skirmish with the French Spahis in the Ahaggar.

Not until I had sent the jewelled seat to England, through an Arab merchant whom I knew in Algiers, and it was exhibited before a meeting of the Royal Geographical Society, was I aware of its real antiquarian value. From the letters sent home by the intrepid Dr Chatteris, and still preserved in the archives of the Society, it appeared that during 1839 Salman, the great Sheikh of Aujila, assembled a formidable following, and proclaiming himself Sultan of Tunis, led an expedition through the country, extorting money from the people by reason of horrible tortures and fearful barbarities. While sentencing his unfortunate victims, he always used a curiously-shaped judgment-seat, which, for ages, had been the property of the Sultans of Sokoto, and it thus became known and dreaded as the Throne of the Great Torture, it only being used on occasions when he sentenced the unfortunate wretches to torture for the purpose of extracting from them knowledge of where their wealth was concealed.

Against this fierce rebel the Bey of Tunis was compelled to send a great expedition, and after several sanguinary encounters at Sinaun, and in the Um-el-Cheil, he was utterly routed and killed in his own stronghold at Aujila. Dr Chatteris, in the last letter received from him, mentioned that he had secured the jewelled throne, but that on account of the superstitions of the Arabs it was an extremely difficult matter to convey it to the coast.

Fearing lest he should lose it, he had apparently buried it, and soon afterwards unfortunately fell into the hands of the Sultan of Borku, who held him captive until his death.

Khadidja is still living in Idelès, where she is happily married to the younger son of the Governor, but in the seclusion of her harem she is still in ignorance that, by the curious little souvenir with which she rewarded me, she added to England's national collection of antiquities a valuable and highly interesting relic.

Visitors to the British Museum will experience but little difficulty in finding it, for in the Oriental section at the present moment one of the most frequently inspected and greatly admired treasures is the quaint, historic, and bejewelled Throne of the Great Torture.

The End.

Milton Keynes UK
Ingram Content Group UK Ltd.
UKHW042145281024
450365UK00010B/639